P. T. BARNUM

Other titles in the **Americans—The Spirit of a Nation** *series:*

ABRAHAM LINCOLN
"This Nation Shall Have a New Birth of Freedom"

ISBN-13: 978-0-7660-3170-8
ISBN-10:   0-7660-3170-5

CLARA BARTON
"Face Danger, But Never Fear It"

ISBN-13: 978-0-7660-3024-4
ISBN-10:   0-7660-3024-5

EDGAR ALLAN POE
"Deep Into That Darkness Peering"

ISBN-13: 978-0-7660-3020-6
ISBN-10:   0-7660-3020-2

FREDERICK DOUGLASS
"Truth Is of No Color"

ISBN-13: 978-0-7660-3025-1
ISBN-10:   0-7660-3025-3

JIM THORPE
"There's No Such Thing as 'Can't'"

ISBN-13: 978-0-7660-3021-3
ISBN-10:   0-7660-3021-0

MATHEW BRADY
"The Camera Is the Eye of History"

ISBN-13: 978-0-7660-3023-7
ISBN-10:   0-7660-3023-7

AMERICANS
THE *Spirit* OF A *Nation*

P. T. BARNUM

"Every Crowd Has a Silver Lining"

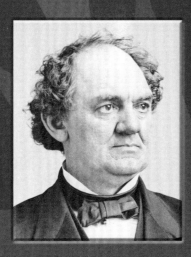

Tom Streissguth

Enslow Publishers, Inc.
40 Industrial Road
Box 398
Berkeley Heights, NJ 07922
USA

http://www.enslow.com

Library of Congress Cataloging-in-Publication Data

Streissguth, Thomas, 1958–
    P. T. Barnum : "every crowd has a silver lining" / Tom Streissguth.
       p. cm. — (Americans : The Spirit of a Nation)
    Includes bibliographical references and index.
       Summary: "Explores the life of showman P. T. Barnum, including his start as an
    entrepreneur, creating the American Museum, building and losing his fortune, and
    introducing the three-ring circus to America"—Provided by publisher.
    ISBN-13: 978-0-7660-3022-0
    ISBN-10: 0-7660-3022-9
       1. Barnum, P. T. (Phineas Taylor), 1810–1891—Juvenile literature. 2. Circus
    owners—United States—Biography—Juvenile literature. I. Title.
    GV1811.B3S77 2009
    791.3092—dc22
    [B]
                                                2008017442

Printed in the United States of America

10 9 8 7 6 5 4 3 2 1

To Our Readers:
We have done our best to make sure all Internet Addresses in this book were active
and appropriate when we went to press. However, the author and the publisher have
no control over and assume no liability for the material available on those Internet
sites or on other Web sites they may link to. Any comments or suggestions can be sent
by e-mail to comments@enslow.com or to the address on the back cover.

♻ Enslow Publishers, Inc., is committed to printing our books on recycled paper. The
paper in every book contains 10% to 30% post-consumer waste (PCW). The cover
board on the outside of each book contains 100% PCW. Our goal is to do our part to
help young people and the environment too!

Illustration Credits: Associated Press, pp. 6, 114; Barnum Museum, Bridgeport,
Connecticut, pp. 14, 15, 18, 49, 64, 94; Enslow Publishers, Inc., p. 12 (bottom); Getty
Images, pp. 52, 58, 81, 89, 97, 105, 112; The Granger Collection, New York, pp. 22,
25, 27, 42, 71, 86; Library of Congress, pp. 3, 10, 12 (top), 33, 44, 54, 62, 68, 76, 84,
91, 101, 102, 107, 111; © Norbert Rehm, Shutterstock.com, p. 40; © Tom Grundy,
Shutterstock.com, p. 9.

Cover Illustration: Library of Congress (portrait of P. T. Barnum).

CONTENTS

P. T. Barnum

Chapter

1

A Hoax

With his father and grandfather trailing behind him, Phineas Taylor (P. T.) Barnum stumbled through the desolate marsh. Brambles and poison ivy clutched at his legs. Angry hornets buzzed around his head. His feet ached, and his shoes were covered with mud and slime.

He pushed on, determined to reach his destination: Ivy Island. This little estate near his home in Connecticut was his own private patch of land, his to keep forever. He often heard about Ivy Island, but he had never seen it—until now.

For ten years, his grandfather, also named Phineas, had been telling P.T. about it, using words that made young Phineas envious. Meanwhile, the rest of the family asked him, in serious tones, about his intentions. Would he raise a home on his lush country acres, or use Ivy Island as a private hunting preserve? Would he sell the land to start a business, or just pass it on to his lucky heirs?

P.T. had not resolved the question. After all, he was only twelve years old. The title to Ivy Island would not belong to him until he became an adult.

He knew only one thing: He was lucky to have such a clever and generous grandfather. The elderly man had made the gift as a way of saying "thank you!" He appreciated his daughter Irene and his son-in-law, Philo Barnum, using his name for his first grandson. He deeded the land to young Phineas when the boy was only two years old.

Now P.T. would finally explore his private domain.

A Jokester Grandfather

There were many things P.T. admired about his grandfather. The old man was talkative and funny, and he loved to play jokes. He had a way of telling stories that grabbed you. They were fascinating stories, until you realized the entire tale was an outrageous lie.

Phineas always seemed to have a plan or scheme in mind. He ran a lottery, selling the chance for riches to local people. He was a good businessman and knew how to strike a deal. And he loved his practical jokes. Much later, P. T. Barnum wrote that "My grandfather would go farther, wait longer, work harder and contrive deeper, to carry out a practical joke, than for anything else under heaven."[1]

Ivy Island's Secret Revealed

The day was getting late, but P.T. kept slogging. Finally, his grandfather and father could not hold back.

They called a halt and gave P.T. the news. This swamp, this reed-choked marsh, this worthless stretch of nothing at all, was Ivy Island. P.T. could walk for as many miles as he wished. He would never reach his promised lush estate—as he was now standing in the middle of it. His grandfather had tricked him.

His grandfather's laughter could be heard for quite some distance. As he grew into a young man, and started out in a business of his own, P.T. never forgot its cheerful, mocking sound.

Ivy Island was named after the poison ivy that covered it. P. T. Barnum did not find this out until the joke was on him.

2

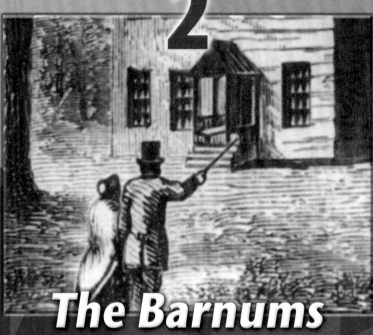

The Barnums of Bethel

The Barnum family had lived in southwestern Connecticut since the 1600s. Philo Barnum was an innkeeper, storekeeper, and farmer in the town of Bethel. He was not rich, but he owned some land. He went to church every Sunday. He was a friendly man.

His first son, P.T.—for Phineas Taylor—was born on July 5, 1810. P.T.'s first memory came from the War of 1812. He remembered watching Bethel's militiamen training on the village green.[1] The British were coming again to fight the Americans, and these volunteers were preparing to defend their town. While he was growing up, P.T. often heard Revolutionary War stories from a proud veteran, his grandfather Phineas Taylor.

P.T. began his studies when he was six years old. His father hired a tutor to teach math and other subjects. The tutor found that young Barnum had a flair for writing and telling stories.

P.T. also had a good head for business. While still in school, he worked in his father's general store. He bought and sold groceries, liquor, and other items. He bartered when customers came with their own goods to trade. Some asked for credit—to pay for their purchases later. Some paid their loans back, some did not.

P.T. quickly learned the ins and outs of trade, money, and profit. He moved to another general store in Grassy Plain, a place not far from Bethel. But the general-store business soon bored him. It was just too easy and predictable. P.T. needed a challenge. He loved to talk and negotiate. He wanted bigger risks and better opportunities.

Starting Out

Philo Barnum died in 1826, when P.T. was only fifteen years old. The family was now without its father, protector, and breadwinner. Worse, Philo had left only debts and no money at his death. P.T. later described the dark day: "the world looked dark indeed . . . [we] returned to our desolate home, feeling that we were

P. T. Barnum was born in Bethel, Connecticut, in the home pictured in the drawing above.

The World of P. T. Barnum

forsaken by the world, and that but little hope existed for us this side of the grave."[2]

Bethel was getting too small. P. T. Barnum felt a need to set out on his own. He traveled to Brooklyn, New York, where Oliver Taylor, a relative of his mother, hired P.T. to work in his store. It was good to live in a city and meet new people every day.

But P.T. did not care much for his job. He was not the kind of man to simply earn a salary every week and scratch by on a small budget. He loved business and taking chances. He loved to wheel and deal, and get the better side of every transaction.

Old Phineas came to the rescue. He invited his grandson back to Bethel. P.T. could use a carriage house, if he would use it to set up a business. In May 1828, P.T. opened his own store in Bethel. He sold fruit, vegetables, candy, ale, and household goods. He called it the Yellow Store. Barnum wrote:

> *I drove many a sharp trade . . . with old women who paid for their purchases in butter, eggs, beeswax, feathers, and rags, and with men who exchanged for our commodities, hats, axe-helves, oats, corn, buckwheat, hickory nuts, and other commodities . . . I asked and obtained the privilege of purchasing candies on my own account, to sell to the juvenile portion of our customers.*[3]

Then P.T. discovered the lottery business. There were many lottery companies all over the nation. Agents sold lottery tickets to the public. The agents worked out of stores and small offices. They earned a

Barnum's mother was named Lena.

small commission for each ticket they sold. But they sold nothing unless they advertised and convinced people to try their luck.

P.T. had a talent for promotion. He named his lottery office the Temple of Fortune. He printed handbills and posters and talked up the lottery to customers. He told them stories of incredible luck, and made a few exaggerations to the local newspapers.

For a chance to earn much more, people gladly paid fifty cents or a dollar (a sum worth about twenty-five dollars in modern money). On some days, P.T. sold more than a thousand dollars worth of lottery tickets—a grand sum of money.[4]

Meeting Charity

Chance sent P.T. good luck one day, when Charity Hallett came to his shop. She was a seamstress from the town of Fairfield, and about two years older than P.T. The sight of her, P.T. later wrote, "sent all sorts of agreeable sensations through my bosom. I was in a state of feeling quite new to me . . ."[5]

Charity and P. T. Barnum fell in love at a very young age.

Taking a Chance

In P. T. Barnum's time, lotteries were a big business all over the nation. In some towns, they were the only way to raise money for new buildings and roads. But some of the lotteries were scams. Lottery officials paid only a small part of the money they promised. In the 1820s, the state of New York became the first to ban lotteries. By 1905, lotteries were illegal everywhere in the United States. They did not return for sixty years.

The day was stormy, so P.T. offered to bring her back home safely to Bethel. That night and over the next few days, Barnum could not forget Charity's kind and friendly face. Although he had an offer to move to Tennessee and run an even bigger lottery, P.T. turned the offer down. He did not want to move away quite yet.

P. T. Barnum and Charity soon fell in love. In the summer of 1829, Barnum asked her to marry him.[6] When Barnum's family heard the news, they did not approve. Charity was only a seamstress, and her family was not of a high social class. Barnum paid no attention to his family's complaints. One day in November 1829, he told his family he had a business appointment in New York. He brought Charity with him to the city, where they were married in the home of her uncle, Nathan Beers.

Strong Views on Religion

Barnum had strong views on the subject of religion. The state of Connecticut had an established church, the Congregational Church. Every resident paid taxes to support the church. The pastors of the church played an important role in politics. Some of them won election to the state legislature, where they wrote and passed laws.

Barnum felt strongly that church and state should be completely separate. He believed that citizens should be allowed their own views. They should attend the church of their choice. Despite Connecticut's history as a colony founded by religious leaders, there should be no established church.

> **Barnum felt strongly that church and state should be completely separate.**

When Barnum read articles in the Danbury newspaper favoring the establishment of the church, they made him angry. But when he wrote letters to the editor to protest, the newspaper did not publish them.

The editors would never allow his views into print. After all, he was a Universalist—someone who believed all Christian sects were equally valid. In Connecticut, such a person lost many of his legal rights.

The *Herald of Freedom*

Barnum knew of another way to get his views into the public eye. In the fall of 1831 he founded Bethel's first newspaper, the *Herald of Freedom*. Like many papers of

This is the front page of an early issue of Barnum's weekly paper, the Herald of Freedom, *which earned him a jail sentence.*

the day, it was just a folded sheet, four pages long. It carried advertisements, opinions, and a few news articles. For the most part, it served as a forum for the opinions of P. T. Barnum. Barnum's paper attracted wide attention. The "establishment" controversy was raging. Some people favored an established church in Connecticut. Others—the "disestablishmentarians"—opposed it. They believed that the U.S. Constitution banned establishment in the First Amendment: "Congress shall make no law respecting an establishment of religion, or prohibiting the free exercise thereof . . ."

While Congregationalist pastors thundered from their pulpits, Barnum and other disestablishmentarians thundered right back in newsprint and brochures. One of his sharpest rivals on the subject was his own uncle, Alanson Taylor. For a time, Taylor even edited a rival newspaper, the *Danbury Recorder*.[7]

Taylor was a die-hard Congregationalist. He and P. T. Barnum took turns taunting and attacking each other in print. At one point, Taylor even sued his nephew for libel.

A Pleasant Turn in the Bethel Jail

Barnum enjoyed the controversies raised by his newspaper. But one day in 1832, he described a wealthy Bethel citizen, Seth Seelye, as a "hypocrite" in the *Herald of Freedom*. He also accused him of usury— the crime of making loans at a very high rate of interest.[8]

Seelye charged Barnum with libel. The charge did not much bother Barnum. If found guilty, of course, he could go to jail. He was willing to take his punishment for the sake of some publicity.

That is exactly what happened. He was tried in a local court. As a Universalist, he was not allowed to testify on his own behalf. He was found guilty, and sentenced to a fine of one hundred dollars and two months in jail.

Many people sympathized with Barnum and believed he was being singled out for persecution because of his stand on religion. Barnum himself wrote: "The excitement in this and the neighboring towns is very great, and it will have a grand effect. *Public opinion* is greatly in my favor . . . I chose to go to prison, thinking that such a step would be the means of opening many eyes, as it no doubt will."[9]

> "P. T. Barnum and the band of music took their seats in a coach drawn by six horses . . ."

Barnum experienced a pleasant time in jail. He ate and drank to his heart's content. He edited the *Herald of Freedom* from his cell, which held a small library of books. He received visitors at all hours of the day. People who had never met him sent him gifts to show their support for him.

When the day of his freedom came, a big procession made its way to the jailhouse. A band played and prominent citizens congratulated him. Barnum described the festivities in the December 12, 1832, issue of the *Herald of Freedom*:

> *P. T. Barnum and the band of music took their seats in a coach drawn by six horses, which had been prepared for the occasion. The coach was preceded by forty horsemen, and a marshal, bearing the national standard [flag]. Immediately in the rear of the coach was the carriage of the Orator and the President of the day, followed by the Committee of Arrangements and sixty carriages of citizens, which joined in escorting the editor.*[10]

At the hotel, waiters and cooks laid out a sumptuous banquet in Barnum's honor. A crowd cheered. Many people gave speeches of praise. Barnum himself spoke about standing up for liberty and the right of free speech.

While Seth Seelye was forgotten, Barnum became the most famous citizen of Bethel. He was known all over Connecticut, and beyond. He had a knack for entertaining people and winning them over to his side. Like old Phineas Taylor, he also knew how to convince skeptics and make them believe whatever he said. He would soon be putting this skill to very good use.

Chapter 3

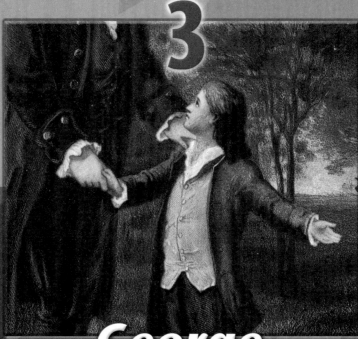

George Washington's Nurse?

For several years, P. T. Barnum worked behind the counters of the Yellow Store. The store made a small profit. Barnum's favorite part of the store was the small desk where he sold lottery tickets. This business required the skill of promotion: talking, promising, and exaggerating. It was salesmanship and showmanship. Barnum was good at both. He also learned about the power of advertising:

> *Fully appreciating the powers of the press . . . I did not fail to invoke the aid of "printer's ink." I issued handbills, circulars, etc., by tens of thousands, with striking prefixes, affixes, staring capitals, marks of wonder, pictures, etc. The newspapers throughout the region teemed with unique advertisements. Immense gold signs, and placards in inks and papers of all colors, covered my lottery office.*[1]

Running the rest of the store was not easy. Barnum had to accept losses when customers who bought on credit did not pay him back. He had to keep records and chase after debts. If the debtor did not cooperate, Barnum had to go to a judge and get an order. Then he had to collect, with the help of the police. The whole process was very bothersome.

Barnum also had problems with Uncle Alanson Taylor. They disagreed over politics and religion, and found it hard to work together, or even hold a normal conversation. When the subject of church and state came up, so did a violent argument.[2]

The American Museum

On May 27, 1833, the Barnums celebrated the birth of their first child, a girl named Caroline Cordelia. The baby girl was healthy and beautiful. Barnum enjoyed the sense of becoming a man of means and responsibility.

But the happy event was soon followed by bad news: Connecticut had made all lotteries illegal. Unable to carry on his most profitable business, Barnum sold his share of the Yellow Store. He prepared to move away from Bethel. There was only one possible destination for a man of his talents and energy: New York City. He moved to the city with his family in the winter of 1834.

Barnum enjoyed New York's noise, traffic, energy, and opportunity. The city was thriving. Hurrying pedestrians and speeding carriages crowded the streets. Ambitious men struck their deals in offices, hotel rooms, restaurants, theaters, and on the streets and sidewalks. Anything could be bought, and it seemed that everything was for sale. All it took to succeed here was a talent for promotion—Barnum's specialty.

Barnum did not want a regular job and a meager salary.

He only needed a good opportunity. Barnum did not want a regular job and a meager salary. He wanted to take risks and make a fortune. He read the papers religiously, scanning the advertisements for his chance. He also announced that he had twenty-five hundred dollars to invest and invited propositions from the public. A flood of ideas arrived in the mail, or in person, and all of them seemed to be a waste of time. One gentleman proposed that Barnum invest all his money in paper and ink—in order to counterfeit money.[3]

One inventor was holding appointments at Scudder's American Museum, at the corner of Broadway and Ann Street. An elderly professor explained to

This engraving by William Henry Bartlett shows a view of New York City from Weehawken, New Jersey, around 1840, only a few years after Barnum moved to New York City.

Barnum that he had developed a "hydro-oxygen microscope." It would be one of the most valuable scientific instruments ever made. To manufacture his creation, the professor needed one thousand dollars immediately. He also asked for a future payment of another thousand dollars.[4] Barnum turned him down.

He did not know much about microscopes, but P. T. Barnum did admire the fascinating exhibits at the American Museum.

Discovering Joice Heth

Money was running short. In May 1835, Barnum opened a boardinghouse, where people could rent rooms from him. He then went into partnership with a New

York businessman named John Moody. They opened a small grocery store on South Street. The shop lay near the wharves on the city's Lower East Side.

That summer, an acquaintance named Mr. Coley Bartram arrived at Barnum's store with some interesting news. Bartram had just sold a slave woman named Joice Heth to a Kentucky promoter named R. W. Lindsay.

Joice Heth was old, blind, unable to walk, and not of much use for work of any kind. But she was believed to be 161 years old. Bartram explained to Barnum that a bill of sale dated 1727 gave her age as 54. Even more interesting, the name on the bill of sale was Augustine Washington, the father of George Washington. Joice Heth, Bartram explained, had been George Washington's nurse. She had been present at his birth and practically raised the boy who would become the first president.

Lindsay had Joice Heth, but he did not have a knack for showmanship. He had bought the rights to exhibit her but had little notion of how to go about it. Now he wanted to part with his rights to Joice Heth for a good price.

Barnum thought it over. New York and Philadelphia newspapers had covered the story. The public knew a little about Joice Heth, but many people had not yet seen her. He decided to see for himself. He boarded a train for Philadelphia.

There Barnum found Heth lying on a couch in a small room. People were paying a small admission fee to file through the room. They were staring while she

Joice Heth claimed that she knew George Washington (right) when he was a boy.

talked and sang. The customers asked her questions to test her knowledge.

She was blind, her teeth were gone, and the fingernails on her wrinkled hands had nails four inches long. But she had a keen memory, and no end of stories about the young George Washington.

Barnum demanded some proof of Joice Heth's age. Lindsay showed him the bill of sale signed by Augustine Washington. The bill was placed under glass. It was faded and torn. It looked genuine enough.

Barnum inspected the document. Though he still did not believe Heth was 161 years old, he agreed to buy the right to exhibit her for one thousand dollars. To raise the money, he sold his interest in the grocery store, and he borrowed five hundred dollars from a friend.[5]

On Tour With Joice Heth

Barnum arranged to exhibit Heth in a room in the private home of William Niblo, a New York restaurant owner. Niblo paid for expenses in exchange for one-half the ticket sales. Barnum hired a lawyer, Levi Lyman, to act as master of ceremonies. Lyman took questions from the curious onlookers.

To spread the word, Barnum printed thousands of handbills and posters. They revealed the astounding story of the ancient Joice Heth in flowery language:

> *JOICE HETH is unquestionably the most astonishing and interesting curiosity in the World! She was the slave of Augustine Washington (the father of Gen. Washington) and was the first person who put clothes on the unconscious infant, who, in after days, led our heroic fathers on to glory, to victory, and to freedom. To use her own language when speaking of the illustrious Father of his County, "she raised him." JOICE HETH was born in the year 1674, and has, consequently, now arrived at the astonishing*
> *AGE OF 161 YEARS*[6]

Barnum gave newspaper editors a few stories about Heth. The editors appreciated these ready-made stories. Such articles made their jobs easier—especially when they came along with advertising, which helped the paper pay its expenses.

The publicity brought in thousands of curious people. Niblo's home was crowded every day, all day. Barnum took in fifteen hundred dollars a week, which he divided with Niblo.[7]

When ticket sales slowed in New York, Barnum took Heth on a tour of New England. There many people opposed slavery. Barnum promised to use the money from ticket sales to buy the freedom of Heth's five great-grandchildren, who were still slaves in Kentucky.

But Joice Heth was in poor health. When she became ill, Barnum sent her to Bethel, and

The examination of Joice Heth did not go so well for Barnum.

asked his half brother, Philo, to care for her. Heth died on February 19, 1836. Barnum had already promised David Rogers, a New York doctor, that he would be allowed to examine Heth if she died. The autopsy took place on February 25 before an audience of physicians and newspaper editors. Barnum charged fifty cents for admission.[8]

The examination of Joice Heth did not go so well for Barnum. Rogers declared that she could not have been more than eighty years old. The *New York Sun* ran an exposé of the Heth hoax. The New York papers published interesting details about the fraud, including the fact that the 1727 bill of sale mentioned the "state" of Virginia. In 1727, Virginia was still a British colony.

Barnum tried to defend himself, but the public was not buying it. The newspapers were growing skeptical, too. Barnum protested that he had been the victim of a hoax and swindled at the hands of R. W. Lindsay.

Barnum had made some enemies.

No matter. Barnum knew all along that no human lives to be 161 years old. He may not have been completely honest. Some even called him a trickster, a deceiver, a "humbug." But he had amazed and entertained thousands of people. He had made a small fortune from Joice Heth and—better yet—his name was in all the papers.

But Barnum had made some enemies. The newspaper editor James Gordon Bennett had published several pieces in his *New York Herald* on the subject of Joice Heth. He also published a story claiming that Joice Heth was still alive, and living in Connecticut, and that Rogers had dissected the body of another woman. The story had been fed to him by Levi Lyman. It was a complete lie.

When Bennett realized he had been tricked, he erupted in anger. He would never forget how Barnum and Lyman had made a fool out of him. From that point on, he used the *Herald* many times to expose Barnum's hoaxes and deceptions. As for Barnum, he saw the newspaper stories about him as a useful means of getting publicity for his acts.

In later years, Barnum wrote a book entitled *Humbugs of the World.* He saw "humbug" as an important part of business and of society, one that was common to many walks of life:

> *Business is the ordinary means of living for nearly all of us. And in what business is there not humbug? 'There's cheating in all trades but ours,' is the prompt reply from the boot-maker with his brown paper soles, the grocer with his floury sugar and chicoried coffee, the butcher with his mysterious sausages and queer [odd] veal . . . all and every one protest each his own innocence, and warn you against the deceits of the rest. My inexperienced friend, take it for granted that they all tell the truth—about each other!*[9]

The Jugglers

Barnum brought Joice Heth to towns large and small all over New England. While traveling, he kept on the lookout for his next exhibition. When he arrived in Albany, New York, he discovered Signor Antonio.

Signor Antonio could balance plates on the ends of sticks, which he held up by his nose. He could keep plates, bowls, and cups spinning and dancing to music. He could also stand on stilts while holding up bayonets by the sharp tips of their blades.

Barnum hired Signor Antonio for a modest weekly salary. He changed the performer's name to Signor Vivalla, which he thought had a more exotic ring. In New York, Signor Vivalla made his debut at the Franklin Theater. For the first time, Barnum himself appeared on stage, to hand the performer his plates and other props. Signor Vivalla was a hit.

In Philadelphia, however, Vivalla ran into a hostile crowd. In the middle of his act, people in the audience hissed and heckled. As his plates wobbled uncertainly in the harsh glare of the stage lights, the people shouted out insults and laughed at him.

Shocked, Barnum challenged the hecklers to identify themselves. They were friends of a local juggler, J. B. Roberts. Barnum threw down a public challenge: He would reward J. B. Roberts or anyone else who could copy Signor Vivalla's act with a prize of one thousand dollars.[10]

J. B. Roberts read Barnum's challenge in the newspaper. He realized that he had to respond. But when he arrived to negotiate the performance with Barnum, he discovered that Barnum expected him to duplicate Vivalla's entire act, feat for feat.

No juggler could precisely duplicate the tricks of another. Each trick took years of practice and used the juggler's particular abilities. Even an expert like Roberts would probably need months to master Vivalla's tricks.

Roberts tried to back out. Barnum had nothing to gain by showing up Roberts. But he knew that he could still hold a competition between the two men.

Barnum arranged the contest. Signor Vivalla and J. B. Roberts appeared together, offering the audience two acts for the price of one. Barnum advertised the event in all the newspapers, and passed out thousands of handbills to advertise. The public could not resist.

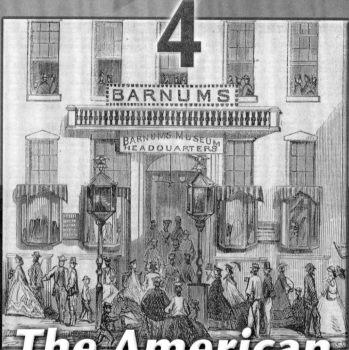

The American Museum

As the crowds for his jugglers, J. B. Roberts and Signor Vivalla, began to thin, Barnum left town and hit the road with a traveling show known as the Columbian Circus. The circus showcased clowns, magicians, equestrians, and Signor Vivalla. The owner, Aaron Turner, hired Barnum as treasurer and ticket seller. In exchange for his work, Barnum earned 20 percent of the profits.

For the next two years, Barnum traveled with a variety of shows. It was a hard, uncertain life.

He often had very little money. Charity stayed in New York, as life with a traveling show was not suitable for a woman with a young child. Barnum wrote to her often, telling her that he missed his family.

At Vicksburg, Mississippi, he sold off his horses and wagons for a steamboat, which he sailed downriver to New Orleans. When he arrived in the city, he found he had no way of moving his exhibits and performers anywhere.

Barnum grew fed up with the constant struggle. Not only was he poor, but he was also a long way from home. After he returned to New York, he tried some new stage ventures, but made no money from them. In the meantime, his family was growing—his second daughter, Helen, was born on April 18, 1840.

He never doubted his talents as a showman—but he was beginning to doubt his chances of making a living at it. In the fall of 1841, a gentleman from back home in Danbury contacted Barnum. He was owed money for some land Barnum had purchased. He did not have much faith in Barnum's future. He wanted the money paid back, immediately.

Barnum had no money. He was working as a clerk for the Bowery Amphitheater, and just getting by. It was time for action.

Making a Deal

In need of money, Barnum searched for a good opportunity. For several days he scanned the papers, and found nothing of interest. Then he heard about the American Museum.

Barnum had wandered its halls before. The museum stood at Broadway and Ann Street. It held thousands of curiosities. There were stuffed animals, insect specimens, fossils, wax

Barnum saw the chance he had long been waiting for.

figures, pictures, coins, medals, and historical exhibits. There was a small lecture hall on the ground floor.

The museum had been losing money for a long time. The owners wanted to sell. Barnum saw the chance he had long been waiting for. Frederick Olmstead owned the land, and John Heath was responsible for the museum. Their price for the building and the collection was fifteen thousand dollars.

Barnum wrote to Olmstead with a proposal. He had no money to offer, but he did have enough talent and energy to make the museum a success. Olmstead could keep possession of the property, while Barnum paid for the museum out of ticket sales. Barnum offered ten thousand dollars. When Olmstead and Heath turned him down, Barnum raised his offer to twelve thousand.[1] He made another offer: If he failed to make his payments, the men could keep any money he had paid them. They could then sell the museum to someone else.

Olmstead and Heath finally agreed. There was one catch. Olmstead wanted security—property he could claim should Barnum fail to live up to his part of the bargain. Barnum offered him five acres of Connecticut land known as Ivy Island. Olmstead eagerly agreed.

Barnum felt certain the American Museum would be his. But on the day he arrived to sign the papers, Heath gave him some bad news. The New York Museum Company also wanted the American Museum—they had offered full price, fifteen thousand dollars, and paid Heath a deposit of one thousand dollars to seal the deal. Barnum was out of luck.

A Little Trick of Business

John Heath wanted the best offer he could get for the American Museum. Barnum had not offered the asking price, and he had not yet signed any agreement. In about six weeks, the New York Museum Company would become the new owners of the American Museum.

Barnum discovered that a group of speculators owned the New York Museum Company. The speculators had little interest in running a museum. Instead, they just wanted to make some money. They planned to sell fifty thousand dollars worth of shares in the museum to the public. They would earn thirty thousand dollars from the stock. The stockholders would run the museum and the speculators would make a big profit no matter what happened.

Barnum worked out a new plan. He told John Heath that he would hold to the agreement he had already made. He would come back on December 27, the day after the New York Museum Company would have to pay the balance of fourteen thousand dollars. If Barnum's rivals failed to come up with the money, then Heath would sell the museum to him.[2]

Heath agreed. Barnum had Heath put the agreement into writing, swore him to secrecy, and then went to work. He called on his many friends in the newspaper business. He wrote articles about the New York Museum Company, telling the public about the stock swindle the men were cooking up. The newspapers were happy to print the articles. Barnum had bought advertising space from them before—if he succeeded in buying the American Museum, he would probably buy much more.

The directors of the New York Museum Company were not happy about the articles Barnum was writing. Nobody was buying their museum stock.

> **They called Barnum into their office and made him a generous offer.**

They called Barnum into their office and made him a generous offer. He could work for them, as manager of the American Museum. They would pay him a salary of three thousand dollars a year.[3] He could start on January 1, 1842. There was only one condition—he must stop writing newspaper articles about them.

Barnum happily agreed. He told nobody about his plans.

Museum Mogul

Barnum was counting on the directors of the New York Museum Company. He was depending on their laziness. They thought the museum was theirs, and that Barnum posed no threat.

When December 26 came, the directors were nowhere near the offices of John Heath or Frederick Olmstead. They would take their time in making the final payment. They had little to worry about—

they had no rival for the American Museum. Or so they believed.

Barnum arrived in the office of John Heath promptly at 9:30 on the morning of December 27.[4] He spent a few hours happily signing papers, then sent a short letter to his rivals in the New York Museum Company:

GENTLEMEN—
It gives me great pleasure to inform you that you are placed upon the Free List of this establishment until further notice.

P. T. BARNUM, Proprietor[5]

The New York Museum Company was taken by surprise. They threatened to take Heath to court. But they had violated the terms of their agreement with Heath by not paying him promptly. They had to accept their fate. However, Barnum would allow them to visit the museum any time they wished, without charge.

Barnum's Museum

Barnum moved Charity and his children into a ground-floor apartment inside the American Museum. Then he set to work. He purchased and designed hundreds of new exhibits. He depended on the public interest in exotic things and curiosities. One of his first special exhibits was a scale model of Niagara Falls. The model showed cliffs, trees, and buildings. A pump and barrel created the illusion of a magnificent waterfall, with water dropping eighteen inches to the rocks below.

Barnum announced his exhibit in a newspaper advertisement:

THE GREAT MODEL OF NIAGARA FALLS, WITH REAL WATER![6]

Thousands of customers paid their quarters, curious to see how Niagara Falls could be contained within the walls of the American Museum. When they arrived at the exhibit hall, they saw a small stream of water flowing gently over the top of a miniature cliff and down into a basin.

Soon after the exhibit opened, Barnum received a stern letter from the Croton Water Commission. The commission was charging him only twenty-five dollars a year for the use of water for the entire museum—if Niagara Falls was to be a part of the museum exhibits, it would have to charge more, much more. Barnum faced down the commissioners, and in his words, "I explained the operation of the great cataract, and offered to pay a dollar a drop for all the water I used for Niagara Falls exceeding one barrel per month, provided my pump continued in good order! I was permitted to retire."[7]

Barnum tripled the receipts of the American Museum in its first year under his management. He soon paid off all his debts to Frederick Olmstead. The success of the American Museum drove its main competitor, Peale's Museum and Portrait Gallery, completely out of business. Peale's displayed a great variety of birds, animals, plants, and other natural curiosities, including the bones of a woolly mammoth.

Barnum recreated Niagara Falls in his American Museum. People flocked to see his version of such a majestic feat of nature. However, they soon found out that his model was smaller than they had imagined.

But Barnum's more spectacular wonders, and his flair for show business, drew a much bigger public.

Barnum had energy, shrewd business sense, and a talent for promotion. He knew what would interest the public. First of all were his human curiosities, such as William Henry Johnson, also known as Zip or "What-Is-It?" Johnson had a strange twisting gait, a double set of teeth, and a head in the shape of a cone. According to Barnum's pamphlets, he had been captured in the wilds of Africa. He was, Barnum claimed, the missing link between humans and their distant ancestors. The claim, however, was false.

The "Aztec" children Maximo and Bartola had tiny heads and were supposedly captured in Central America. There were albino families, such as the Lucasies, a father, mother, and child. They had no pigment in their skin and looked completely white. There were "leopard-spotted" African-Americans, whose skin was spotted white, a condition known to modern doctors as vitiligo. Barnum brought fifteen American Indians of the Sac, Fox, and Iowa tribes east from the Great Plains. The Indians performed war dances, simulated hunting parties, and demonstrated scalping techniques.

Controversy surrounded the human exhibits. Critics accused Josephine Fortune Clofullia, the Bearded Lady, of being a man, a charge she denied in the company of her husband. (Barnum himself had orchestrated the accusations, in order to raise the public's interest.) She later appeared at the museum with a baby, the "Infant Esau," to prove her gender. Esau himself already seemed to have a full beard and whiskers at the age of two.[8]

Barnum got people to accuse his bearded lady of really being a man.

Drawing Crowds

Barnum invested the museum profits in improvements. He changed the drab exterior of the museum with a coat of bright, fresh paint. He had artists paint large oval portraits of exotic animals, which were placed between the windows on the upper stories. The oval paintings were put on in a single night, for maximum effect.

> *I never before saw so many open mouths and astonished eyes. Some people were puzzled to know what it all meant; some looked as if they thought it was an enchanted palace that had suddenly sprung up; others exclaimed, "Well, the animals all seem to have 'broken out' last night," and hundreds came in to see how the establishment survived the sudden eruption.*[9]

Flags flew from the balconies and roof. At night, bright lights shone down on Broadway, lighting up the street north and south for blocks. Banners spread across the lower floors advertised the latest, strangest exhibits. Hawkers passed out handbills on the street and invited customers inside.

If the bills and posters could not draw in customers, bad music might. A small brass band, made up of six poorly trained musicians, tooted from the museum's front balcony. The noise was shrill and unpleasant; the only way to escape it was to move along or pay for a ticket to come inside.

Barnum had agents all over the world scouting for the museum. The agents sent reports of oddities, exotic animals, and strange-looking humans. If he felt

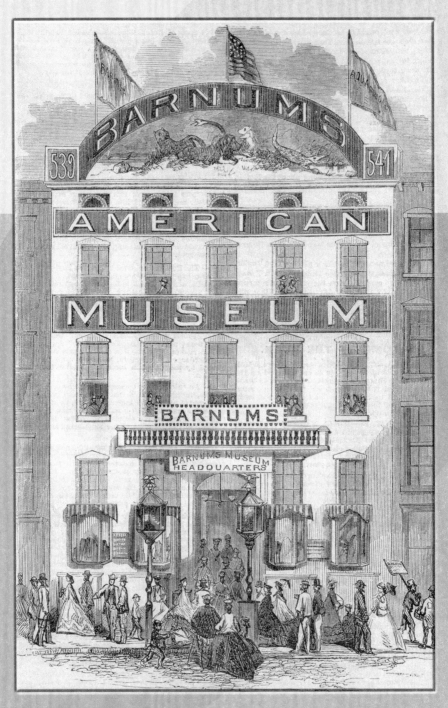

Barnum's new American Museum was located on Broadway in New York City, between Spring and Prince streets.

interested, Barnum offered money to bring the exhibit to the museum.

When he heard of something strange or marvelous, Barnum quickly took advantage of public interest with an imitation. "Caspar Hauser" was advertised as a genuine nature boy, raised by wild animals. The idea for this exhibit was borrowed from the real Kasper Hauser, a boy who had lived on his own in a German forest, and who had died in Germany in the 1830s.

The museum also had a marketplace. Men and women wandered the halls, selling their goods to the customers. A phrenologist examined the bumps on people's heads to read their character and predict their future. Fortune-tellers read tarot cards. Taxidermists stuffed and mounted dead pets brought in by visitors. The museum offered a shooting range in the basement, and a picnic area on the roof for customers to relax in the fresh air.

Barnum repaired the museum's famous Lecture Room. Every afternoon and evening, the Lecture Room held a show. On holidays, when the museum was full of customers, there were performances every hour: magic-lantern shows, magicians, jugglers, ventriloquists, singers, musicians, and comedians. There were contests of skill, dogs that did tricks, and clowns in their costumes and makeup.

Barnum's Lecture Room was a place for families to enjoy a spectacle. In that time, women or children did not attend ordinary theaters, which were often dirty, dangerous places with rowdy drunks, bad behavior onstage and in the audience, and fistfights. In the

American Museum, Barnum strived to set a higher standard. He commissioned plays from local writers and staged the works of famous authors from Europe. There were temperance plays that dramatized the dangers of alcohol and abolitionist plays about the evils of slavery.

Contests also drew in paying customers. There were dog shows and beauty contests. Photographs of the contestants were placed on public view. Museum-goers voted for "finest twin," "finest triplet," and the "finest baby."[10] The museum exhibited some of the winning babies for a few days. The contests brought crowds of interested people but also some trouble, when mothers with losing children grew angry and difficult to handle.

At the exit, the museum offered patrons free prints of the exhibits. People brought them home to show friends and family, who grew curious themselves to see the exotic collections. Nearly every tourist or casual visitor to New York crossed the threshold into the American Museum and Barnum's strange and fascinating world.

The Fiji Mermaid

It was some time in 1843 that P. T. Barnum first heard about the Fiji Mermaid. It turned out to be one of the strangest exhibitions he ever placed before the public.

A sailor from Boston had found the Fiji Mermaid while ashore in the port of Calcutta, in British India. According to his story, he had purchased the mermaid for six thousand dollars.[11] Without enough money of

Barnum's Buffalo Hunt

At times the Lecture Room and the museum did not provide enough room for acts inspired by Barnum's fertile imagination. Seeing an opportunity in the fascination for the Wild West, Barnum once hired the owner of a small buffalo herd to stage a buffalo hunt. The hunt would take place in the wilds of New Jersey, just across the Hudson River from New York, where a group of men dressed as American Indians would track wild buffalo through the brush.

Unfortunately, the show was not a big success. As the crowd gathered, a small herd of young buffalo appeared in a small field, calm and very tame. The buffalo stood around and did nothing. The derisive laughter of the crowd did more to frighten them than the guns of their make-believe hunters.

For Barnum, however, the attraction was a success. Although he earned nothing from ticket sales, he did make money by selling refreshments. He also took a percentage of the money made by the ferry that brought his customers across the Hudson.

his own, the sailor had stolen money from his own ship's treasury to obtain the mermaid. He had taken her on a tour of Europe and Asia, and had failed completely. He spent the rest of his life working to pay back the large sum of money he had stolen from his own ship, with only a mermaid to show for his efforts.

The sailor had died without a penny or any property—except for the Fiji Mermaid. His son had no interest in keeping his strange inheritance. He sold it to Moses Kimball, proprietor of the Boston Museum. Kimball brought the mermaid to New York and to his friend P. T. Barnum. When Kimball arrived in Barnum's office, the two men unwrapped the object and studied it closely. On Barnum's desk was the dried up, mummified body of a monkey, skillfully sewn onto the tail of a fish. In Barnum's own words, "the animal was an ugly, dried-up, black-looking and diminutive specimen, about three feet long. Its mouth was open, its tail turned over, and its arms thrown up, giving it the appearance of having died in great agony."[12]

It was one of the most repulsive things Barnum had ever laid eyes on. But P. T. Barnum appreciated nothing so much as a challenge. His task was to raise the public interest, bit by bit, until the curiosity of newspaper editors and the people reached a fever pitch. Then, and only then, would the Fiji Mermaid appear in the halls of the American Museum.

As Barnum well knew, the natural world still held many mysteries. Unknown places were still being explored. New species were constantly coming to light. The amazing discoveries of scientists filled many

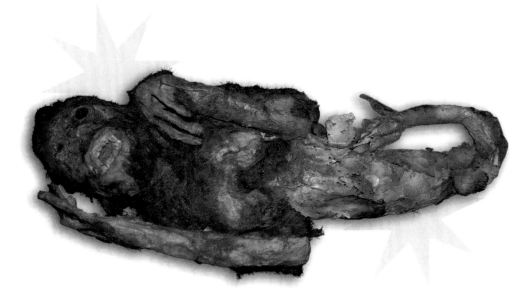

The original Fiji Mermaid has been preserved in the Peabody Museum of Natural History, in Cambridge, Massachusetts. This photo is of the replica at the Barnum Museum.

columns in the newspapers. But scientists did not know everything, and they were often proved wrong. Who could say what might be a hoax—and what might be absolutely true?

Barnum had a plan for the Fiji Mermaid. He had friends around the country mail letters to New York newspapers. The letters mentioned Dr. Griffin from the Lyceum of Natural History in London, who had arrived in America with a very strange object. The doctor would be coming to New York, ready to exhibit the specimen to anyone interested.

By the time "Dr. Griffin" got to New York, the newspapers were eagerly waiting for him. Barnum hired his old friend and colleague Levi Lyman to play the part of Dr. Griffin. Lyman had been the master of ceremonies at the exhibition of Joice Heth. Barnum now engaged him to play an even bigger and better role.

Barnum announced that he was interested in buying the object from Dr. Griffin and giving it a permanent home in his museum. To show he was sincere, he had even prepared an engraving of the mermaid as well as a written description. The Fiji Mermaid appeared as a beautiful, beguiling, half-fish half-woman. She was drifting in the sea, eluding a band of sailors eager to capture her.

Dr. Griffin then announced he was turning down Barnum's offer. But he sent Barnum's engraving and description "exclusively" to three different newspapers. The papers published Barnum's account all on the same day. By the end of that day, the entire city of New York was talking about the Fiji Mermaid.

Barnum printed pamphlets describing the Fiji Mermaid and rushed them out to the public. The demand for the exhibit grew stronger. Dr. Griffin finally gave in to the impatient clamor. He agreed to exhibit the Fiji Mermaid at a New York concert hall for a limited engagement—one week only. Then he moved the exhibit to the American Museum. Posters appeared throughout the city, showing the Fiji Mermaid as a beautiful siren of the sea.

Thousands rushed in the halls of the museum to the special glass case where the mermaid was laid to rest. Some were disappointed at the sight of a dead monkey sewn to the tail of a fish. But their tickets allowed them to explore the entire museum, and attend a show in the Lecture Hall.

After public interest in the Fiji Mermaid died, Barnum placed the object in a box, which he kept in his office. He later donated it to another museum. He may have felt a little shame at the hoax.[13] But he was quite a bit richer because of it.

Chapter 5

General Tom Thumb

In late 1842, P. T. Barnum visited the city of Bridgeport, Connecticut. A friend had told Barnum about the young Charles Stratton. He was four years old, the son of a carpenter and the youngest member of a working-class family who lived in an ordinary neighborhood. He was a normal boy in every way—except for his size. He was a very small boy.

At first, Barnum was skeptical. By this time, people from all over were trying to convince him to invest in their curiosities. He knew that many of them were simply trying to fool him and steal his money.

P. T. Barnum had seen everything, or so he thought. On entering the Stratton house, Barnum found himself astonished. Young Charles was less than two feet tall and weighed no more than sixteen pounds.

Barnum hired Stratton and his father on the spot to appear at the American Museum. He returned to New York and began to introduce Charles Stratton to the public. He adopted the name of a hero of English folktales, and planted stories about "General Tom Thumb" in the newspapers. His advertisements claimed that Stratton was an eleven-year-old English boy. On December 8, 1842, General Thumb made his premiere.

Barnum signed a contract with the Strattons and offered a salary of three dollars a week.[1] Charles Stratton's parents would be responsible for taking care of the boy. Mr. Stratton was also expected to do some odd jobs and carpentry whenever he might be required.

Tom Thumb attracted thousands of people to the American Museum. He appeared in costumes and uniforms on the stage of the Lecture Hall, which Barnum decorated with miniature furniture and a large dollhouse for the little person's use. During the show, the boy struck poses from familiar statues, told jokes, and conversed with the audience. He played characters from history, including Napoleon, the short French general. He impersonated sailors, aristocrats, and professors.

After his appearance at the American Museum, Tom Thumb toured the eastern United States. Audiences

Tom Thumb stands next to P. T. Barnum. Thumb was one of Barnum's main attractions for years.

filled concert halls and theaters to gawk at him and enjoy his act. As more people saw him, interest began to wane. Barnum knew it would not be good to expose Tom Thumb too often to the American public. If luck stayed with him, Stratton would remain small for many years.

Barnum decided to send Stratton on a European tour. Early in 1844, the Strattons and Barnum sailed for England. Before he left, Barnum arranged to have his own letters published in the *New York Atlas*. In the letters, he would describe his adventures and Tom Thumb's success. The letters would keep public interest in Tom Thumb alive.

Meeting the Queen

The rough crossing of the Atlantic Ocean took nineteen days.[2] Tall waves rolled constantly underneath the ship. It was hard to walk, to stand, even to sleep. But P. T. Barnum had no problem with rough weather and the high seas. He roamed the decks, speaking with passengers and the crew of the ship. He laid his plans for Tom Thumb's conquest of England. After the boat docked in the port of Liverpool, Barnum had Mrs. Stratton wrap Tom Thumb in baby clothes and carry him to a hotel. He did not want anyone to see the little person yet.

When they arrived in London, the capital of England, Barnum rented an expensive house in the West End, a high-class neighborhood. He allowed people to visit by invitation only. They might come from the richest, most powerful families in England—they still

> **"After dinner we saw the greatest curiosity I, or indeed anybody, ever saw . . ."**
>
> —Queen Victoria

needed a personal invitation. For a fee, people could also have Tom Thumb visit their own homes. Wealthy families in London competed to have the boy entertain them at dinners and parties.

As public curiosity about Tom Thumb grew, Barnum devised another plan. He knew Queen Victoria herself loved to see exotic animals and curiosities from all over the world. Barnum called on the American ambassador, Edward Everett. He asked Everett to speak with the queen and interest her in a "command performance."

Everett agreed to the idea. Queen Victoria had already read newspaper stories about Tom Thumb. She officially commanded Barnum and Tom Thumb into her presence. On March 23, Barnum and Tom Thumb put on their best clothes and rode in a carriage to Buckingham Palace. The queen and her court were delighted. They especially enjoyed Tom Thumb's Napoleon—the French general had fought a long, costly war against the English, just one generation before.

The queen led Tom Thumb around the palace by the hand, and proudly showed off her paintings and possessions. That night, Queen Victoria gave an account of the meeting in her diary:

After dinner we saw the greatest curiosity I, or indeed anybody, ever saw, viz: a little dwarf, only 25 inches high & 15 lbs in weight. No description can give an idea of this little creature, whose name was Charles Stratton, born they say in 32, which makes him 12 years old. He is American, and gave us his card, with Gen. Tom Thumb written on it. He made the funniest little bow, putting out his hand & saying: "much obliged Mam." One cannot help feeling very sorry for the poor little thing & wishing he could be properly cared for, for the people who show him off tease him a good deal, I should think. He was made to imitate Napoleon & do all sorts of tricks, finally backing the whole way out of the gallery.[3]

The queen invited Tom Thumb back to the palace several times. She introduced him to her family; princes and princesses happily crowded into the audience hall to watch him sing, tell jokes, and do imitations. The king of Belgium and the czar of Russia arrived to shake his hand.

Barnum realized that he had to keep up appearances. He bought a special suit of court clothes for Tom Thumb. He also had a carpenter build a miniature carriage. The part of the carriage where Tom Thumb sat was just twenty inches high, and was drawn by four miniature ponies. Whenever Tom Thumb made his formal appearances, children in costume rode on the outside of the carriage, which had windows fitted in the front and sides so that Tom Thumb himself was easy to see by crowds lining the streets.

Trouble With the Strattons

Barnum and the Strattons toured France and the European continent. Barnum found more exhibits and

Tom Thumb steps out of a carriage that was specially made for him.

curiosities for the American Museum: bell-ringers; a "Happy Family" of different animals, all living together in the same cage; and a letter-writing automaton—a machine in the form of a human, operated by a man hidden within.

In Stratford-upon-Avon, about seventy-five miles northwest of London, Barnum offered to buy the boyhood home of William Shakespeare. He meant to take it apart and bring it back to the United States. But the English resisted. They did not want this American showman taking away a national landmark, the very house where their greatest writer was born and raised. A group of men bought the house and donated it to the Shakespeare Association. The house remained in Stratford-upon-Avon.

The Barnums and the Strattons returned to New York in October 1844. Barnum's third child, Frances, had died just before her second birthday. His wife, Charity, wanted him home. The weeks and months when he was away in England were hard and lonely, but he did not stay long in America. In November, he brought his wife and his two daughters aboard another transatlantic ship.

On his second trip to Europe, Barnum enjoyed Paris and France even more than England. In the capital of Paris, Tom Thumb was a smash hit. As "Tom Pouce," he appeared before the king of France. In his miniature carriage, he rode through the streets to the acclaim of adoring crowds. The French countryside made Barnum happy, and he described it in a letter to his friend Moses Kimball: "This is a most *charming* country, & he who has not seen it has seen *nothing*. . . . There is no ale here, but I guess there is a little *w[ine]* . . . It's a great country, Moses, & you *ought* to be here a month with me—but there's no use talking, you won't come . . ."[4]

His family was happy to see the sights and travel with Barnum. But the Strattons were trying to tell Barnum how to promote their son. They were also demanding more money.

Barnum agreed to pay them more. After all, Tom Thumb's appearances were making enough for everybody. There was good reason to avoid problems—Charles Stratton was still a child, and his parents had the final say in his career. If they wanted to, they could simply bring him home, put him in a regular school, and offer him a normal life. But Barnum would not give up any responsibility for promoting the act. Advertising, promoting, arranging exhibitions and performances—that remained his job.

The Strattons grew more demanding. "The Strattons are crazy," wrote Barnum in a letter to a friend:

> [A]bsolutely deranged with such golden success. At first they were inclined to take airs, carry high heads, and talk about what we were doing; but when she thought expenses were too high and that I spend too much for printing, etc, I told them both very decidedly *that I was the* manager *and that unless the* whole *was left to my direction [I] would not stay a single day.*[5]

This quickly put an end to the demands.

Iranistan

By the mid-1840s, Barnum had enough money to build the home of his dreams. He bought seventeen acres in Fairfield, Connecticut, just west of Bridgeport. Hundreds of workers swarmed over the site, raising a fanciful mansion on the rolling, tree-shaded grounds. Barnum named the house Iranistan.

Barnum modeled his fanciful new home on the Royal Pavilion, an elaborate public hall at the seaside resort of Brighton, England. His new home was made of sandstone, and it reached ninety feet to the top of its highest dome.[6] It looked like a sultan's palace. The name "Iranistan" was Barnum's idea of lending the home an exotic touch.

Under the central dome of the main building was a huge room with a circular sofa big enough for fifty people. Iranistan had dozens of smaller outbuildings, including stables for horses, greenhouses with exotic trees, and storehouses for Barnum's small fleet of carriages. An artificial pond stocked with fish was built at the rear.

Inside, there were antique furniture, tall fireplaces made of marble, and thick Oriental carpets. Hot-air furnaces kept the house cozy on cold nights. Gas lights illuminated all of the rooms. The dining room could seat several dozen people, and a luxurious billiard room was available for the guests. In all, the house and grounds cost Barnum the astounding sum of one hundred fifty thousand dollars (equal to about $4.2 million today).

Barnum's mansion Iranistan was located in Fairfield, Connecticut.

The tour had made the Strattons wealthy. But as the money came in, it was quickly spent. Cynthia Stratton, Tom Thumb's mother, bought expensive dresses and jewelry. Her husband began drinking and became an alcoholic. Tom Thumb was subjected to a difficult life as a human exhibit. He had no young friends. Instead of going to school, he took private lessons with a tutor. He moved in an adult world, dressing up and telling jokes for the amusement of paying customers. He was never free to play and explore the world on his own, as other children did.

The Teetotaler

Although he had enough money to retire, Barnum did not allow himself to lead a life of ease. He remained the director of the American Museum and held to a very strict daily schedule. He rode the train into New York every day and spent most of his time at the museum. He received visitors at the Astor House, an elegant nearby hotel. In the late afternoon, he returned to Iranistan, his hilltop mansion. At home, he spent much of his time writing letters and reading books.

Charity Barnum had been worried about her husband's hard work and his time away from home. His drinking also had been a problem. On many days, Barnum began drinking early in the afternoon. On some days he came home in a bad mood, and was ready for an argument with his wife. He often ignored his daughters, including the youngest, Pauline, who was born in the spring of 1846.

In the summer of 1847, the problem grew worse. Barnum himself began to realize that he had to make a change. One night he found himself exhibiting Tom Thumb in the town of Saratoga Springs, New York. The show went well, but the sight of so many drunkards in the audience brought him to an important decision.[7] He would try to give up alcohol.

He spent a difficult time trying to live up to this pledge. The pressures of the job, and the frequent dinners and parties, kept him drinking. He raged at his wife, and the frequent criticism of him by her mother, Hannah.[8] Their home grew tense and unhappy.

In 1848, while hearing a sermon by a Universalist minister, Edwin Chapin, Barnum swore to give up drinking. That same night, he went into his cellar, uncorked dozens of champagne bottles, and poured

Barnum quit drinking after making a promise to his family. From the left are Barnum's daughters: Caroline, Pauline, and Helen.

them out on the ground. He then signed a temperance pledge. He promised his wife and family to never touch alcohol again.

The Swedish Nightingale

The happy crowds still passed through the front doors of the American Museum. For Barnum, the business was a gold mine. (In 1852, he would sign a new lease on the building—for twenty-five years.)

His reputation as a successful showman pleased Barnum. But many called him a humbug and a hoaxer. Some pointed out that the Fiji Mermaid and Joice Heth were nothing more than tricks. The criticism made Barnum angry. He wanted people to see him as a serious man, not a humbug.

In Europe, he found a new kind of act to bring to the American public. She was a star of serious music, a singer who drew huge audiences wherever she appeared. Her name was Jenny Lind.

Jenny Lind sang with a beautiful, pure voice. Many people thought they heard the sound of a nightingale as they listened. She could sing high and low tones, and hold a note for as long as a minute. Her voice could be heard in every corner of the largest halls of Europe. She sang popular songs as well as arias, songs taken from long musical dramas known as operas.

Lind was known for her good works as well as her singing. She spent much of her money on charities, such as hospitals and orphanages. She mingled with workers and the poor as much as with the nobility and the wealthy. She was deeply religious, devoted to her faith and a regular churchgoer.

When Barnum heard her sing, he knew he had to bring her to the United States. She would be the "Swedish Nightingale," a new kind of act, and no hoax or trick.

For Lind, however, he had to invest money—a larger sum than he had ever invested before in a single act. She agreed to sing 150 concerts in the United States, for a fee of one thousand dollars per appearance.[9] She asked Barnum to pay everything he owed her in advance, before she arrived in the United States. He would also have to pay her musical director and a fee for another singer who appeared with her. He would have to pay for all her expenses, including transportation, meals, and hotel rooms.

Barnum was wealthy, but he had trouble raising enough money to bring Jenny Lind to America. He had to mortgage his home, Iranistan, and also take a loan on the American Museum. In the end, he even had to borrow money from his friends.

Barnum did not hesitate. He knew that with good promotion, Jenny Lind would be a success, and he would earn his entire investment back very quickly.

An American Tour

Jenny Lind had read a few newspaper stories about P. T. Barnum and the interesting curiosities he had exhibited in America. She saw herself as a serious musical performer—an artist, not a freak of nature. She hesitated before agreeing to sign Barnum's contract.

Then Barnum sent her a note on his personal stationery. The stationery showed Iranistan, Barnum's fanciful house. To design and build such a beautiful palace, in Lind's eyes, showed that Barnum was a man of taste and means. She finally agreed to sign.

Barnum prepared for Jenny Lind's tour. He arranged hotels, rented out concert halls, and hired ticket agents in every city in which Lind was to appear. He ran advertisements and placed newspaper articles. He organized a Jenny Lind Prize Song Contest, with a two hundred dollar prize for the best poem to be set to music, just for Lind.[10] He sent biographies of Lind to the newspapers, as well as his own letters describing her training, her musical style, and her personal life. This made it easy for the newspapers to fill their pages. In return, Barnum calculated, they would give Lind favorable reviews.[11]

Barnum sometimes employed his daughter Caroline to serve as Jenny Lind's double.

The singer arrived in New York aboard the *Atlantic* on September 1, 1850. A great crowd gathered at the dockside. People lined the streets and cheered her entourage as it made its way to her hotel. In New York and in every other city she appeared, people crowded train platforms, concert hall doorways, hotel lobbies, and the streets.

In some places, the press of the mob proved too much for Jenny Lind. She often refused to appear in public,

Jenny Lind became a national sensation during her time in the United States.

fearing the great commotion. Barnum sometimes employed his daughter Caroline to serve as Jenny Lind's double.[12] The real Jenny Lind would hide while the crowd dispersed, then stroll in peace to her destination.

The entire country went crazy for Jenny Lind. She became a superstar, her face appearing on posters throughout the country and her every move described in the newspapers. People paid huge sums of money for tickets to her concerts. In important cities, the first tickets were always auctioned off to the highest bidder. Wealthy people across the country bid for the honor of holding the first ticket in their town for a Jenny Lind concert.

In every city, Barnum happily staged one sold-out concert after another. He bore all the expenses and still made a spectacular profit. He even paid for the cost of staging concerts for charities. The proceeds went to benefit orphanages, hospitals, and rest homes. He lost money at the charity concerts. But he was happy to bear the burden, as he knew such events would only bolster his own reputation.

The End

Despite the success of Jenny Lind, Barnum himself grew weary of the demands of the tour. He was rushing from one place to another, solving problems and dealing with Lind's helpers, friends, and agents. The constant demand for his time, attention, and money exhausted him.

During a tour of towns along the Ohio River, unruly crowds upset the singer on several different nights. She blamed Barnum for the problems, and finally asked him to cancel the tour. Barnum realized that the public was losing interest in Jenny Lind. He agreed to tear up their contract in June 1851, when the tour was two-thirds finished.

Lind then found herself responsible for her own management, and all the petty annoyances that Barnum had been dealing with. She did not have Barnum's talent for promotion, and her concerts were far less successful. Lind continued touring for another year. In May 1852, she gave her last concert at the Castle Garden music hall in New York City, the place where she had made her American debut.

By this time, she had worn out her welcome with the critics. The reviews turned negative, and the public lost interest. Jenny Lind returned to Europe, still friends with P. T. Barnum. In the ninety-five concerts he had managed, he had taken in a gross (before expenses) amount of more than $700,000 (over $19.3 million today). Jenny Lind herself had earned $176,000 (over $4.8 million today).[13] It was the most successful concert tour in American history up until that time.

Money Trouble

In 1851, P. T. Barnum formed a partnership with Seth B. Howe and Lewis Lent. The three men staged a traveling exhibition called Barnum's Caravan. The show's biggest attraction was a group of ten Asian elephants, the most ever gathered in North America up until that time.

Barnum eventually retired one of the elephants to Iranistan, where he installed a small field of crops. To advertise his shows, he had a worker hitch a plow to the elephant, who lumbered back and forth in plain view of commuters on the nearby New Haven Railroad.

New Ventures

Barnum was on the lookout for new ways to make money. He had a shrewd eye for public taste in entertainment and tireless energy. He knew how to invest his money wisely, or so he believed. Money invested in a good cause, in his opinion, would benefit him the most.

In the fall of 1851, Barnum went into partnership with William H. Noble, a Bridgeport lawyer. Noble owned fifty acres of land that he had inherited from his father.[1] The land lay east of the Pequonnock River, just outside the city limits of Bridgeport.

Barnum paid twenty thousand dollars for a half interest in the venture. He wanted to keep the business a secret, for now. He and Noble quietly bought 174 more acres of land.[2] They began raising a new city, East Bridgeport. They laid out streets and parks, and built new homes, schools, shops, factories, and a bridge to Bridgeport across the Pequonnock River. When the homes and other buildings were ready, Barnum and Noble offered them for rent.

Barnum was on the lookout for new ways to make money.

The rents from the properties allowed the partners to pay their expenses. But the real profit came from a rise in the value of the improved land. The partners held half of the building lots in East Bridgeport off the market. As residents moved in, businesses started operating, and the lots became more valuable. Barnum and Noble then sold the lots.

Barnum also made a good profit from his own life story. His autobiography *The Life of P. T. Barnum, Written by Himself* was published in 1854. It described his childhood and his rise to wealth and fame in New York. The book was filled with stories from behind the scenes at the American Museum. Readers by the millions eagerly bought the book. Barnum released new editions every few years. The book remained a bestseller for decades.

Bankruptcy

When he made a business decision, Barnum relied on his experience and instincts. He felt he could do no wrong. This was especially true if his investments were for a good purpose, such as providing jobs for the residents of East Bridgeport. In 1854, he invested in the Ansonia Clock Company and brought the company to his new city. The company was renamed the Terry and Barnum Manufacturing Company.

Soon afterward, a representative of the Jerome Manufacturing Company of New Haven came to Bridgeport. Chauncey Jerome, the president of the company, was the biggest maker of clocks in Connecticut. He sought to merge his company with Barnum's.

Barnum accepted the offer. The Jerome Manufacturing Company would take over Terry and Barnum. Chauncey Jerome promised that his company would move to East Bridgeport. In exchange, P. T. Barnum would get stock in the new company. He also had to pledge one hundred ten thousand dollars worth of security in order to cover the company's expenses and debts. Barnum put Iranistan and other property into the deal as security.

Barnum signed dozens of promissory notes, which pledged payment to banks, suppliers, and other creditors. Within three months, he had signed notes for one hundred ten thousand dollars of the company's debts.

> **Barnum had received one of the worst shocks of his life.**

According to the agreement with Chauncey Jerome, that amount was the most he could possibly owe. Sure of his success, Barnum did not bother to keep track.

Barnum was an optimist—he believed in himself and trusted others. But in a short time he was in debt for almost five hundred thousand dollars.[3] The Jerome Clock Company turned out to have more debts than property, more expenses than income. Without enough money or property to back up his promises to pay, P. T. Barnum went bankrupt.

All the money he had spent on the Jerome Clock Company had gone to pay off old debts. He knew nothing about these debts when he first signed the deal with Chauncey Jerome. The company did not have enough money for operating expenses. It finally closed its doors in 1856—without ever having moved to East Bridgeport.

Barnum had received one of the worst shocks of his life. He had to start his life all over again. He mortgaged Iranistan and leased it to his half brother Philo Barnum. He moved his family out of the mansion and back to

New York City, where they lived in a rented house on West 8th Street.

Charity Barnum fell into a deep depression. Unhappy in New York, she fell victim to many illnesses, some of them real and some of them imagined.[4] To restore her to health, Barnum sent her to a farm in Westhampton, Long Island. There she could rest and take in the fresh air and the peaceful views of Long Island Sound.

For the next few years, Barnum spent many of his days in court. He had to face creditors and explain how he would repay the promissory notes he had signed. Many people came forward with claims against him. Several even tried to cheat him, by presenting notes that had already been paid. Barnum himself grew depressed and anxious.

The End of Iranistan

The lack of money did not bother P. T. Barnum. In his view, money could always be earned. What angered him was the sight of an unpleasant side of human nature—the greedy side that would do anything to profit from the bad luck of another.

Barnum's enemies swooped down on him like hungry vultures. Newspaper editors, including James Gordon Bennett, declared the showman had gotten what he deserved. The great humbug, who had put forward so many frauds and hoaxes, was now paying the price for manipulating the public. Many people hoped that the

This photo of P. T. Barnum was taken between 1855 and 1865.

Jerome Clock Company had put an end to Barnum's public career. In his memoirs, Barnum wrote:

> *I was taken to pieces, analyzed, put together again, kicked, 'pitched into,' tumbled about, preached to, preached about, and made to serve every purpose to which a sensation-loving world could put me. Well! I was now in training, in a new school, and was learning new and strange lessons.* [5]

Slowly, Barnum dug himself out of debt. He managed to settle most of the promissory notes. He transferred property to his wife so that the courts could not seize it. He was able to keep the American Museum open for business and prepared to move back to Iranistan.

In December 1857, Barnum hired workmen to renovate the mansion. He wanted it to be more beautiful than ever, inside and out. By November, the house was almost ready. One evening, workers were cleaning under the big central dome. While leaving the house for the night, one of them left a burning pipe in the room. A few hours later, Iranistan was in flames. Water pumps were still scarce on the property. The entire mansion quickly burned to the ground.

"The Art of Money Getting"

Barnum took the loss of his beautiful mansion in stride. The last few years had taught him an important lesson. He paid less attention to business deals, profits and losses, and new investments. Money did not mean so much anymore. He had so much less of it to worry about.

Barnum saw his bankruptcy as a stroke of good luck. It allowed him to see things in a different light. His pursuit of money had brought a nasty fall. He found more peace and contentment in his poverty than he ever had as a wealthy man. In a letter to William H. Noble, he wrote: "I humbly hope and believe that I am being taught humility and reliance upon Providence, which will yet afford a thousand times more peace and true happiness than can be acquired in the din, strife, and turmoil, excitements and struggles of this money worshiping age."[6]

> "I humbly hope and believe that I am being taught humility . . ."

The people who wished Barnum ill would be disappointed. He returned to London in 1858. He wrote a lecture that he called "The Art of Money Getting." With jokes and amusing stories, taken from his own experience, he talked about the nature of business and how to succeed. He advised listeners to follow their vocation, concentrate their energies, and advertise. Of course, he also provided the audiences with some entertainment. There was music and an exhibition of the Fiji Mermaid.

Every night, the talk ended with a standing ovation. Barnum took "The Art of Money Getting" on the road. He delivered the lecture in more than one hundred towns, earning a good fee for his talk every night. The money he earned from the lecture helped him pay off his debts. When he returned to the United States, he presented "The Art of Money Getting" to new audiences.

He took up a new lifestyle in a new home. He built a smaller house near the sight of Iranistan, and called the new place Lindencroft. The house was comfortable, but it was hardly the imposing monument that Iranistan had been. Inside, the Barnums lived more simply. The showman devoted more of his time and money to charity and the causes of temperance and abolition. He sold the contents of the American Museum to his partners Greenwood and Butler, but continued to work as a manager.

In March 1860, he announced that he had bought the museum back. After more renovations, the building reopened—bigger than ever. Barnum still lived by an important principle: Always give the public their money's worth.

The Commodore in the Walnut Carriage

Meanwhile, General Tom Thumb was growing taller and fatter. He eventually reached the height of three feet. He was definitely no longer a boy. He sported a thin moustache and enjoyed smoking thick cigars. By the time of the Civil War, his act drew smaller audiences. He no longer toured much, and Barnum did little to promote his act. Tom Thumb was in danger of becoming just another human curiosity wandering the corridors of the American Museum.

Meanwhile, news of another little person reached P. T. Barnum. This person was even shorter than Charles Stratton. George Washington Morrison Nutt, the son of a New Hampshire farmer, stood just twenty-nine inches tall. Quietly, without letting the newspapers know, Barnum met Nutt in December 1861 and convinced him to sign a contract to join the American Museum.

The agreement paid Nutt and his brother Rodnia the sum of twelve dollars a week, plus 10 percent of the sales of all souvenirs of their act the museum happened to sell.[7] Their rate of pay would increase every year for the next four years.

After he signed the contract with Nutt, Barnum immediately went to work on the New York newspapers. He planted stories with several editors about "Commodore" Nutt, and revealed that he was in hot pursuit of Nutt's services. According to Barnum's story, he had hired an agent named Fordyce Hitchcock to journey north to New Hampshire. Hitchcock's job was to convince Nutt and his family to sign with America's most famous showman. According to the newspaper stories, Barnum had instructed Hitchcock to offer thirty thousand dollars, or a wage of two thousand dollars a week, to make sure that the commodore would appear only on his stage.

The stories were nonsense, but they served their purpose. His show-business rivals eagerly bid for Nutt, hoping in vain to outmaneuver Barnum. He gleefully reported the details, knowing that Nutt was his act for at least the next five years. In the meantime, the

P. T. Barnum stands with Commodore Nutt in this photo from the early 1860s.

public's curiosity about Commodore Nutt rose to a fever pitch.

Barnum made preparations for the new act. He ordered new costumes for Nutt as well as stage props and furniture. He also had a carpenter design a carriage for Nutt, in imitation of Tom Thumb's. The carriage was built in the shape of a walnut, with its top half opening on a hinge to reveal the small Nutt inside.

Soon New York and Washington, D.C., were talking about Barnum's new little person. President Abraham Lincoln invited Barnum and Nutt to the White House. The tall and gangly president shook hands and joked with the compact Commodore Nutt.

In 1862, Barnum discovered Mercy Lavinia Warren Bump, a twenty-one-year-old schoolteacher from Middleborough, Massachusetts. Bump weighed twenty-nine pounds and stood just thirty-two inches tall. On arrival at the American Museum, she met Tom Thumb and soon fell in love. Eager for a second romance to develop, Barnum introduced Commodore Nutt to Bump's younger sister, Minnie. The commodore and Minnie became friends, but there was no spark of romance between the two.

Soon plans were announced for the grand wedding of Tom Thumb and Lavinia Bump. "The Fairy Wedding" would be a grand spectacle as only P. T. Barnum could put on. Commodore Nutt would serve as the best man, while Minnie Bump was bridesmaid. Barnum had engraved invitations sent out to his guests.

To advertise the event, Barnum sold prints of the couple and displayed Lavinia's wedding gown in the window of a department store. The public closely followed preparations for the ceremony in the newspapers. Attendance at the American Museum skyrocketed.

On February 10, 1863, a crowd of several hundred distinguished visitors ambled through the doors of Grace Episcopal Church. They were the elite of New York: wealthy merchants, officers in the Union army, city officials, theater celebrities, and Barnum's friends and family. They stood up in the church pews to see the couple, perched on small footstools, at the altar.

More than two thousand people attended the wedding reception at the Metropolitan Hotel. Tom Thumb and Lavinia received miniature gifts, including a set of elaborate fire screens sent by President and Mrs. Lincoln. After the reception,

> **More than two thousand people attended the wedding reception.**

they set out on a whirlwind honeymoon through Philadelphia, Baltimore, and Washington, where the president invited the newlyweds to the White House as guests of honor.

The prospects for a world tour featuring General and Mrs. Thumb were too much for Barnum to resist. The pair set out on a three-year tour of Europe, Japan, China, Indonesia, Australia, India, Egypt, the Middle East, and Europe. In 1869, Barnum arranged another tour, this time with Tom Thumb, Commodore Nutt, Lavinia, and Minnie. The four put in three grueling years of appearances, visiting 587 different cities and putting on 1,471 shows.[8]

This photo was taken at the wedding of Tom Thumb and Lavinia Warren Bump. From the left are Commodore Nutt, Bump, an unidentified giant who also worked for Barnum, and Thumb.

By this time, Tom Thumb and Lavinia had adopted a baby.[9] In a few years, the boy towered over his own father.

Barnum sought to give audiences the appearance of a happy family, but he realized that having a son a foot taller than Tom Thumb would be awkward. So, in every town where the couple appeared, the showman arranged to borrow a baby, which appeared with Tom Thumb and Lavinia as if it were their own.

At the end of this whirlwind world tour, Barnum decided he had done all he could for the career of Tom Thumb. The right thing to do, in his opinion, was allow the man to strike out on his own.

The Civil War and Barnum

The country embraced Tom Thumb and Commodore Nutt. Their act was welcome relief in a hard time. The Civil War divided the country in two. Union and Confederate armies fought battles at distant, unknown places such as Gettysburg, Pennsylvania, and Antietam, Maryland. The war called men away from their families to risk their lives and fight for the cause.

An opponent of slavery, Barnum fully supported the Union cause. Not everyone in New York or Connecticut agreed with this stand. The Copperheads in the North opposed the war and believed southern states had the right to keep slavery within their borders. The American Museum became a target of southern saboteurs. Barnum's enemies threatened his life. On some evenings, he posted armed guards outside his house in Bridgeport.

A large crowd gathers as firemen try to put out the fire destroying P. T. Barnum's American Museum on July 13, 1865.

The Great Fire

Fire posed the greatest danger to Barnum's business. There were no public fire departments when Barnum opened his museum. The showman had to rely on his own water and pumping system to guard against a disaster.

Barnum's museum had been a target of Confederate sympathizers throughout the Civil War. In 1864, a plot to burn twelve New York monuments was discovered and stopped. The arsonists had been brought down from Canada by Jacob Thompson, a former member of the presidential cabinet who sided with the South.

On July 13, 1865, arsonists set fires in several different places inside the American Museum. The fire quickly spread. Flames shot from the windows and spiraled above the roof. A huge crowd of curious people gathered on the sidewalks, watching the building burn. Monkeys, polar bears, lions, and kangaroos were trapped inside and burned to death. A seal was dragged out into the street and saved. Parrots, vultures, and eagles flew into the sky from the windows. The arsonists were never caught.

Barnum paid for volunteers to fight in the Union army. At the American Museum, he staged patriotic plays and hired lecturers to speak on behalf of the Union. He also brought Union soldiers and battle veterans to the museum to mingle with the crowds and appear onstage. He joined the Republican Party, the party of President Lincoln.

Barnum became a politician and campaigned for public office. He was comfortable speaking in front of crowds, and he knew how to advertise himself. He was a popular man among ordinary people, workers, and middle-class families. In 1865, voters elected him to the Connecticut General Assembly as a representative from Fairfield.

He won reelection in 1866. He fought with the New York and New Haven Railroad over the exorbitant rates charged to commuters. Barnum also sponsored an amendment, or change, to the state constitution. The amendment would have allowed African Americans the right to vote in Connecticut.

In speaking for the new law, Barnum said:

> *A human soul . . . is not to be trifled with. It may tenant the body of a Chinaman, a Turk, an Arab or a Hottentot—it is still an immortal spirit; and amid all the assumptions of caste, it will in due time vindicate the great fact that, without regard to color or condition, all men are equally children of the common Father.*[10]

Barnum ran for the United States Congress in 1867. His opponent was William H. Barnum, a distant

The Cardiff Giant

In the summer of 1866, George Hull arrived at a small rock quarry near Fort Dodge, Iowa. Hull asked the quarrymen to cut a slab of rock from the ground. Hull brought the slab to the workshop of Edward Burghardt in Chicago. Hull gave Burghardt his instructions and swore the man to secrecy.

Over the next few weeks, Burghardt turned the slab into the figure of a giant. He shipped the giant to his cousin, William C. Newell, in Cardiff, New York. Newell and Hull buried the giant in Newell's backyard.

A few months later, two well diggers working on Newell's property came across the figure of a giant man, somehow turned to stone. The men rushed to Newell's house to give him the news. The story spread like wildfire, and Newell's neighbors arrived by the hundreds to look at the "Cardiff Giant."

Hull charged twenty-five cents per person for people to glance at his discovery. When the crowds began to thin, he sold the Cardiff Giant to a group of men in Syracuse, New York, who exhibited it at one dollar per person. By this time, word of the Cardiff Giant had reached P. T. Barnum, who offered fifty thousand dollars for it. He was turned down.

Barnum ordered his own crew of men to create an imitation. He exhibited his own Cardiff Giant, claiming that the men of Syracuse had sold him the real thing and now were exhibiting a fake. One of the Syracuse men, Mr. Hannum, heard what Barnum was doing, and said, "There's a sucker born every minute!" This went down as the most famous thing that P. T. Barnum ever said—even though *he* never actually said it.

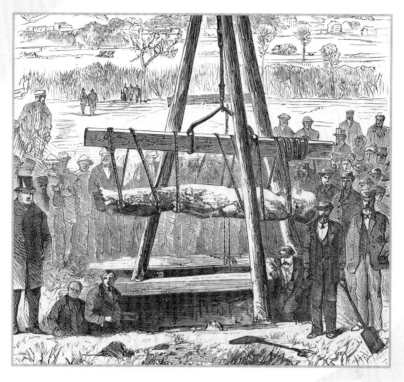

A group of men raise the Cardiff Giant from the field of farmer William C. Newell on August 16, 1869.

relative, from the town of Salisbury. During the campaign, William Barnum was accused in a series of letters of vote buying—paying people to vote for him. P. T. Barnum went on the attack. He wrote newspaper articles, claiming that he would never stoop so low. Rival newspapers attacked P. T. Barnum, and accused him of forging the letters. Was this just another Barnum trick?

The story was trumpeted in the *New York Herald*, owned by Barnum's enemy James Gordon Bennett.

Barnum answered back in the *New York Tribune* (owned by the Republican Horace Greeley). He wrote an eloquent article in his own defense, but the many odd exhibitions and frauds he had brought before the public at the American Museum came back to haunt him. He lost the election by about one thousand votes.

After this campaign, Barnum felt a strong desire to take a rest from the business world. In 1867 he bought a house at 5th Avenue and 39th Street, in New York's fashionable and wealthy Murray Hill neighborhood. He threw his doors open to family, guests, friends, and strangers. Two years later, Barnum and Charity moved into a large house in Connecticut on Long Island Sound. He called the house Waldemere. There were rolling lawns, gardens, fountains, and cottages on the estate for the use of guests.

Barnum soon began working on a book, *The Humbugs of the World*. In its pages, he exposed the many frauds and deceptions carried out by humbugs of the past. A new edition of his autobiography appeared in 1869. He intended to retire from show business and take his leisure. He would attend to his new house and lead a quiet life.

Chapter 7

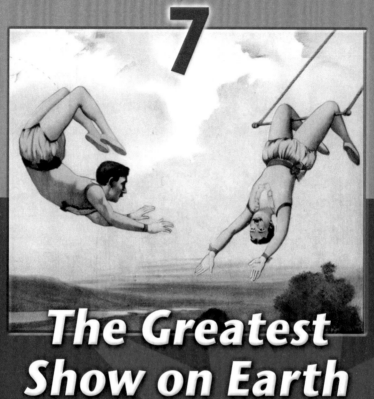

The Greatest Show on Earth

The idle life of a retired businessman quickly bored P. T. Barnum:

Having "nothing to do" I thought at first very pleasant, as it was to me an entirely new sensation . . . But nature will assert herself. Reading is pleasant as a pastime; writing without any special purpose soon tires; a game of chess will answer as a condiment; lectures, concerts, operas, and dinner parties are well enough in their way; but to a robust, healthy man of forty years' active business life, something else is needed to satisfy. Sometimes like the truant school-boy I found all my friends engaged, and I had no play-mate. [1]

Itching to get back into show business, Barnum listened with interest to a business proposition from William C. Coup and Dan Castello. The two partners had formed a circus. In the summer of 1870, they toured the Great Lakes and midwestern river towns on a boat named the *Benton*. Now they asked Barnum to lend his name and invest in a bigger, better traveling circus.

Barnum agreed. He hired performers and bought exhibits, handled publicity, managed the traveling museum, and appeared with the circus when he could. He arranged for circus wagons, chariots, and other vehicles to carry the show from town to town. P. T. Barnum's Grand Traveling Museum, Menagerie, and Circus opened in April 1871.

The show toured New England, New Jersey, and upstate New York. Barnum's name and reputation brought plenty of customers. Show bills were passed out before the circus arrived, while laborers set up huge tents across three acres of land. The circus played to a full house in nearly every town.

For the 1872 season, Barnum dubbed his circus "The Greatest Show on Earth." He put the entire circus on rails. About sixty freight cars, flatcars, and sleeping cars rumbled through the night as the circus moved from town to town. The show moved as much as one hundred miles in a day. In many towns, excursion trains brought customers from far and near to Barnum's ticket booth.

The big top was an immense canvas tent that could hold twelve thousand people. To make it easier for so many people to see his acts, Barnum added a second ring. He also set up a hippodrome track that circled the floor, just in front of the first row. The track was the sight of parades, races, clown acts, and often the grand entrance of P. T. Barnum himself. He sometimes rode atop a carriage and waved to the crowd before the show began.

> **"I yearned to be where I could meet sympathizing friends . . . "**

Keeping the show current and interesting posed a constant challenge. Barnum went on frequent scouting expeditions, always trying to find the biggest, the best, or the weirdest. Money was no object—he spent whatever was necessary to hire the acts he wanted.

On one of these scouting voyages to Europe, in the fall of 1873, Barnum received the sad news that his wife, Charity, had died. On a ship under sail, it took about two weeks to cross the Atlantic—he would never return in time to attend her funeral. "After this sad blow," he wrote, "I yearned to be where I could meet sympathizing friends and hear my native tongue. I therefore returned to London and spent several weeks in quiet."[2] He also met Nancy Fish, the daughter of an English friend, John Fish, while staying at the Fish residence in Lancashire, England.

Nancy was smart and energetic. She wrote books of her own and was a skilled piano player. She brought

P. T. Barnum and his second wife, Nancy, pose at Waldemere shortly after their New York wedding in 1874.

Barnum back to life and made him feel young again. The two were secretly married on Valentine's Day in 1874. Barnum told nobody, not even his closest friends in the United States. He thought it was too soon after the death of Charity. He allowed some months to pass, then sent for Nancy to sail to America. Barnum wanted everything to appear proper. The couple held a formal wedding ceremony on September 16, the day after Nancy arrived.

A New Circus

Barnum's show business did not have much promise when he returned. After he arrived in the United States, P. T. Barnum began a hard time in his life. Audiences for his traveling circus grew smaller. He formed a new company in 1874, the Barnum Universal Exposition Company, in partnership with William Coup and Dan Castello. Barnum wanted to make the circus something more than crowd-pleasing entertainment. He dropped the rings and made the show a hippodrome, with a single large track circling the center arena. The show went on at the New York Hippodrome, which had seats for ten thousand people—the largest indoor arena in the city's history up to that time.

He also went into partnership with John O'Brien, a Philadelphia showman, calling the show Barnum's Traveling World's Fair. This show traveled by wagon train from town to town. The hippodrome show also hit the road. In every town, workers raised a new arena to

Giants of the Museum

Barnum could not get enough of human giants. One of his most famous was Anna Swan from Nova Scotia. She had reached the height of seven feet at the age of fifteen. Barnum hired her to appear in the museum, where she lived in a small apartment. Barnum's guests enjoyed her lectures and often spotted her walking the halls of the American Museum.

Barnum also discovered Colonel Routh Goshen, the Arabian Giant, in the Bowery, a neighborhood near the American Museum. Monsieur E. Bihin, a French giant, was imported to appear in a variety of plays, including *Jack and the Beanstalk*. Barnum put both men onstage with Tom Thumb for comedy acts, and had them stroll through the museum, posing for photographs and raising customers over their heads.

The two famous giants were friendly rivals. One day, however, they appeared to come to blows. When Barnum arrived, they were facing off with a club and a sword. The showman parted the men, saying:

> *Look here! This is all right; if you want to fight each other . . . that is your affair; but . . . if this duel is to come off, I and the public have a right to participate. It must be duly advertised, and must take place on the stage of the Lecture Room. No performance of yours would be a greater attraction, and if you kill each other, our engagement can end with your duel.*[3]

The two men agreed and shook hands. Barnum had planned another winning performance.

Canadian circus performer Anna Swan poses next to her father Alexander Swan (seated) and her mother Ann Haining Swan, a woman of average height in the 1870s.

accommodate a vast crowd. The show required 125 railroad cars and employed twelve hundred people.[4]

Barnum and Bailey

The shows of Barnum's Universal Exposition Company brought in about twenty-five hundred paying customers every night. But the show's profit steadily declined. In 1877, the show made a total of $81,016. In 1878 profits fell to $78,941 and then to $60,357 in 1879.[5] The show was too expensive to move and to operate, and Barnum found himself again dangerously in debt. The economy was poor, and the crowds were growing smaller. William Coup suffered a nervous breakdown and often was absent from work. His partners grew tired of Barnum allowing rival shows to use his name, his image, and his reputation—always for a fee. Barnum eventually quit the partnership.

Meanwhile, in April 1880, James E. Cooper and James A. Bailey brought their Great London Circus and Great International to the city of Philadelphia, Pennsylvania. The circus had something new and special for its audience. Its Indian elephant, Hebe, had just given birth to the first baby elephant ever born in America. Cooper and his partners named the baby Columbia. The public crowded the elephant's stall, eager for a look. Among them was P. T. Barnum.

Barnum knew a great attraction when he saw it. A baby elephant would pack a huge audience into his show tents. He telegraphed a message to the International Circus, offering one hundred thousand dollars for Columbia. Cooper and Bailey turned him down—and then took a page from Barnum's own book and publicized his offer. Now Columbia was not just America's first baby elephant—it was the elephant that P. T. Barnum wanted, but did not have.

Barnum had met his match in business and promotion. If he had owned Columbia, he would have done exactly the same thing. If he could not beat Cooper and Bailey, he would join them. In March 1880, he signed a new agreement with James A. Bailey and James L. Hutchinson.

Bailey had lived and worked in traveling shows since he was a teenager. When Barnum met him, he was a manager and partner with James Cooper in the Great London Circus. This show had toured Australia, New Zealand, Hawaii, and South America. In the United States, it competed directly with Barnum's Greatest Show on Earth. The competition was a drag on ticket sales and profits, for both shows.

In many ways, Bailey was opposite to Barnum, and a different kind of businessman. A quiet and stern man, he did not reveal his real last name to anybody (it was McGinnes).[6] He did not like to put himself in the spotlight. He worried over details and counted every dime. He knew all about every person that his show employed, and every piece of equipment and every animal that it owned. He carefully drew up routes before touring began, and pored over the records of money earned every night.

Almost seventy years old, P. T. Barnum was still keen for money and success. But his health was not so good.

He wanted to rest and enjoy himself. He just wanted to enjoy the fun of show business—finding new acts, planning outrageous publicity stunts, and appearing at the circus from time to time to receive the crowd's applause and adulation. Although they were very different, Barnum and Bailey got along. They were both hardheaded businessmen who did not allow their feelings or their friendship for others to get in the way.

James A. Bailey bought a share of the Great London Circus from James E. Cooper, who retired from the business. Barnum and Bailey took on James L. Hutchinson as their new partner. Barnum invested half of the money, and earned one-half the profits of the show. Hutchinson and Bailey each earned one quarter. Barnum offered his name to the show in all of its banners and advertising. On some nights, he made a personal appearance. He wrote newspaper articles, handled advertising, scouted for new acts, arranged to purchase show animals, and gave advice to his younger partners.

The show set up its winter headquarters in Bridgeport. Performers arrived shortly before the tour began to practice their routines. The entire circus occupied the former crop field near Iranistan, where Barnum had once had elephants plowing the land.

The new show set out in the spring of 1881. It was the largest circus ever seen, and the first three-ring circus in history. A hippodrome track circled the edge of the arena. The sideshow had different curiosities, including General Tom Thumb and the Fiji Mermaid. At night, arc lights powered by a steam generator lit up the rings and the sideshows.

After Barnum and Bailey joined forces, the circus became even more popular.

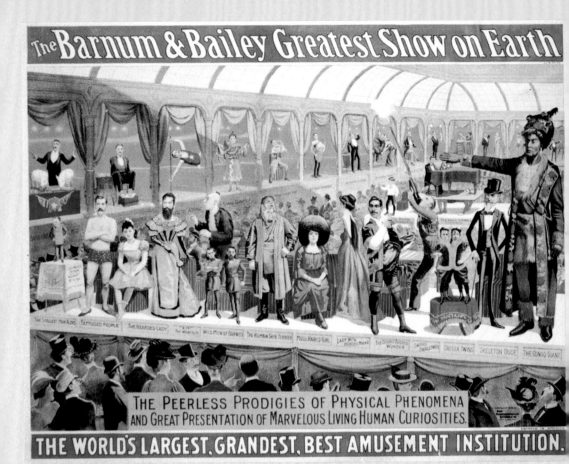

This poster advertising the Barnum & Bailey circus shows the various human oddities that were featured in the show.

The circus moved from town to town by train. In some big cities, the performers held a grand torchlight parade down the main street the night before the show.

Jumbo the Elephant

On his visits to London, Barnum often enjoyed walks through the Regents Park Zoo. He admired animals captured in the wilds of Asia and Africa. Sometimes, he arranged to buy the animals and bring them to America for his shows.

There was one spectacular animal Barnum was sure he would never be able to buy. Standing more than eleven feet tall, and *still* growing, was Jumbo the African elephant. He weighed nearly seven tons, and had big flapping ears and mighty tusks.

Jumbo was the star of the Regents Park Zoo. Children all over England had seen him. A visit with Jumbo was the best part of any trip to the zoo. When they fed him buns and other goodies, Jumbo roared his satisfaction. His trumpet could be heard all over the zoo and throughout the park.

The zoo directors were not so happy with Jumbo. He was expensive to keep. Only one handler could control him. From time to time, Jumbo went on a rampage. He knocked down the walls of his stable and stomped into pieces any heavy fixtures that got in his way. Some day, the directors feared, he would run loose through the zoo, destroying property and hurting people.

When Barnum made his offer to buy Jumbo in 1882, the directors agreed. They sold him for two thousand British pounds—about ten thousand dollars. Barnum would be responsible for transporting Jumbo across the Atlantic Ocean.

The Outcry

The news that P. T. Barnum had bought Jumbo, and would take him to the United States, caused an uproar louder than Jumbo's mighty trumpet. Jumbo was the national pet, almost a symbol of the nation. He represented England's great colonial empire, which, at the time, spanned the world. Now Jumbo, its greatest trophy, was being sold to an American showman, who only wanted to exhibit him in circuses to make money.

The British parliament held a formal debate on the matter. Queen Victoria expressed her disapproval. The newspapers pitched in with sad commentaries on Jumbo's fate. The *London Telegraph* wrote:

> *No more quiet garden strolls, no shady trees, green lawns, and flowery thickets . . . Our amiable monster must dwell in a tent, take part in the routine of a circus, and, instead of his by-gone friendly trots with British girls and boys, and perpetual luncheon on buns and oranges, must amuse a Yankee mob, and put up with peanuts and waffles.*[7]

Barnum was brought into court by several people, who asked that the contract of sale be ruled illegal. Children wrote to the showman with sad pleas; some people wrote with threats against his life. Barnum was offered large sums of money for the elephant so that Jumbo could stay in England. The Royal Society for the Prevention of Cruelty to Animals claimed that Barnum's purchase represented a serious threat to Jumbo's life and health. The *Daily Telegraph* asked Barnum to name his price to cancel the sale. Barnum telegraphed his reply: "Fifty-one millions of American

"Fifty-one millions of American citizens anxiously awaiting Jumbo's arrival."

Jumbo, the famous elephant, resided at Regents Park Zoo in London.

citizens anxiously awaiting Jumbo's arrival. My forty years' invariable practice of exhibiting the best that money could procure, makes Jumbo's presence here imperative. [A] Hundred thousand pounds would be no inducement to cancel purchase."[8]

The reply was published in the *Telegraph* and all over England, drawing huge crowds to the zoo for a last look at Jumbo.

The elephant himself did not seem too keen to move. When he was brought out of his cage, and led to the giant wooden carriage that would bring him to the London docks, he stopped in his tracks. Then he simply lay down on the ground. Nobody could move him an inch. His keeper did not cooperate either, as moving Jumbo to America would mean a big cut in his pay.

Newspaper stories in America and England followed the drama closely, running new stories and pictures nearly every day. Through it all, P. T. Barnum felt a certain glee and satisfaction. The bitter debates, the lawsuits, and even the stubborn Jumbo were just whipping up more publicity. The longer the controversy continued, the more curious the American public would be to see the elephant. Barnum telegraphed the handlers in London, instructing them to let Jumbo lie on the ground just as long as he wished.

After several more days, Jumbo was finally coaxed into his wagon. The vehicle rumbled slowly through the brick streets of London, pulled by a team of ten strong horses. At the shore of the Thames River, he was led aboard the *Assyrian Monarch.* As the boat coasted downstream, thousands of people lined the riverbanks, bidding Jumbo farewell. He would never return.

Jumbo Meets His Match

The *Assyrian Monarch* took thirteen days to reach the United States. On April 8, 1882, the ship docked off Lower Manhattan. A team of horses was assembled, and thick ropes were attached to Jumbo's wagon. Try as they might, the horses could barely move Jumbo into the street.

Elephants were summoned from the circus. They were positioned behind the huge wagon to push it

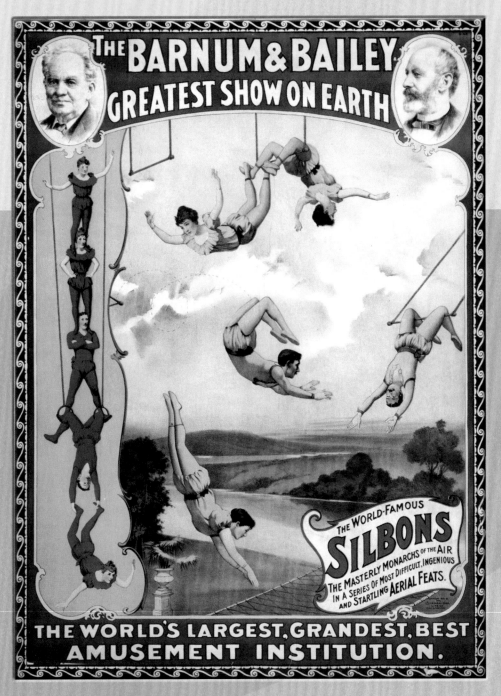

The Barnum & Bailey Greatest Show on Earth poster shows the world-famous Silbons, who were, according to the poster, "the masterly monarchs of the air, in a series of most difficult, ingenious and startling aerial feats."

up the street. The arrival of Jumbo became a grand spectacle, as men, horses, and elephants strained to bring the immense animal uptown.

Buying and moving Jumbo had cost the circus thirty thousand dollars. But the investment very quickly paid off. Jumbo was the most popular exhibit in the history of Barnum's circus. Crowds marveled at the huge beast as he ambled around the hippodrome track, carrying acrobats and trapeze artists, jugglers, and clowns atop the small platform roped to his back. Souvenir stands did a brisk business in Jumbo hats and clothing.

In more ways than one, Jumbo was the biggest exhibit of Barnum's life. But one tragic day in St. Thomas, Ontario, his size became the death of him. On September 15, 1885, he was walking along a train track with a small herd of circus elephants. An unscheduled train came down the tracks. Jumbo's handler tried to coax him down an embankment. The smaller and nimbler elephants quickly got out of the way. Terrified of the slope, Jumbo hesitated.

The locomotive struck the seven-ton elephant. The train derailed and crashed, its cars tumbling off the tracks. Jumbo was pinned under one of the cars. He died soon afterward. "The death of Jumbo was cabled all over the world," Barnum wrote, " . . . I received hundreds of telegrams and letters of sympathy. My first thought was of the many thousands who were counting on seeing the giant beast . . ."[9] Barnum found a solution.

Several museums wanted Jumbo's skin and bones. Barnum himself wrote stories of the elephant's last moments for the newspapers. The circus published a

The White Elephant

After discovering Jumbo in a London zoo, Barnum set himself on an even more difficult mission: to find a "sacred" white elephant in the kingdom of Siam (modern Thailand). Barnum sent an agent to Siam to buy one from the Siamese king. But the king refused to cooperate. The agent then traveled to neighboring Burma, where he bought Toung Taloung for six thousand dollars.

Unfortunately, Barnum had wasted his money. Toung Taloung was not white but light gray, with a pink ear and lighter patches on his skin. White elephants, much to the disappointment of many spectators, were not completely white.

That did not prevent Barnum's rival, Adam Forepaugh, from going Barnum one better. Forepaugh got his sacred beast the easy way: He bought a small elephant in London and simply had him covered with whitewash. The elephant was shipped to New York and exhibited as "The Light of Asia."

When Barnum had his first look, he instantly recognized the trick. He met with reporters in Philadelphia to reveal Forepaugh's deception to the newspapers. Then, never to be outdone by another showman, he ordered his own painted elephant. Through the season of 1884, two rival white elephants appeared before the public.

pamphlet, *The Life, History, and Death of Jumbo,* to promote a new and strange exhibit.[10] Professor Henry Ward of Rochester, New York, spent months preserving Jumbo's skin and bones. Special rolling wagons were built. Jumbo's skeleton was displayed on one, his stuffed and mounted skin on the other. Appearing with him was Alice, a female elephant from the Regents Park Zoo, now billed as his widow. Jumbo remained with his circus, traveling from town to town in the special railway car made for him when he first arrived.

The End of the Show?

A s Barnum grew older, he remained a very busy man. He set up offices in downtown Bridgeport and hired several secretaries to oversee his real estate, his personal finances, and the business of the circus. He put in long days at the office, traveled to distant cities, and wrote books. He also made friends with many famous people, including Mark Twain, Thomas Edison, and President Ulysses S. Grant.

Barnum never stopped collecting exhibits and attending to "show business." In 1884, he organized

Despite being seventy-four years old, P. T. Barnum was still a busy man in 1885, when this photo was taken.

a Grand Ethnological Congress of Nations. He collected people from places he considered "uncivilized," sending agents across the seas to find Polynesians from the South Pacific, Nubians from Africa, Laplanders from northern Scandinavia, Hindus from South Asia, Sioux from the Great Plains, and aborigines from Australia.[1] These and many other people were sent to the United States for public display, promoted by handbills and posters. The Grand Ethnological Congress was one of the most popular features of his circus.

Barnum sometimes worried about being known as a humbug, as many people had called him. So he continued to give large sums of money to charities, to his church, and to the cause of temperance. He donated money to the Bridgeport library, to hospitals and schools, and to Tufts University in Massachusetts, where the Barnum Museum of Natural History was founded.

In 1888, Barnum and his second wife, Nancy, moved into a new home, right next to Waldemere. Barnum installed electric lights, hot running water, and other conveniences. He could not yet settle down, however. In the next year he brought the circus to England, where—despite his purchase of Jumbo—he was treated as a hero. The crowds enjoyed the show and marveled at Jumbo's giant skeleton.

When he returned to America, he settled into his house to read, write letters, and enjoy the company of his grandchildren. In a last letter to James Bailey, he wrote, "You must always have a great and progressive show and also one which is clean, pure, moral and instructive. Never cater to the baser instincts of

Circus clown Molly Pelly works with an elephant before the start of the 133rd edition of the Ringling Brothers and Barnum & Bailey Circus at the Fleet Center in Boston on October 9, 2004.

humanity . . . and always remember that the children have ever been our best patrons."[2] P. T. Barnum died at his home on April 7, 1891. His Greatest Show on Earth survived. His widow sold P.T.'s share of the circus to James Bailey. In 1906, Bailey died, and in the next year the show was sold to John and Charles Ringling, also known as the Ringling Brothers.

The Ringling Brothers and Barnum & Bailey Circus has played thousands of dates into the twenty-first century. The circus still features clowns, equestrian events, high-wire artists, animal acts, and three rings of nonstop entertainment.

P. T. Barnum went down in history as a flamboyant hoaxer. His critics called him a shameless promoter, an opportunist, a fraud, and a humbug. However, his energy and optimism perfectly matched the times in which he lived, when the United States was a growing nation. Through his very creative use of newspapers, he invented modern "show business," where advertisement, promotion, and hype are key. His example has been followed by entertainers ever since, who understand as Barnum did that personality is as much a part of success as talent.

For that reason, Barnum made himself a part of the show. He often appeared at the opening ceremonies of the Barnum & Bailey Circus. The crowd spotted him riding in a carriage, a balding and heavyset man in a dark suit, with no special ability to sing, dance, juggle, or entertain. They instantly stood and burst into applause for P. T. Barnum, the world's greatest showman.

CHRONOLOGY

1810 — On July 5, P. T. Barnum is born in Bethel, Connecticut.

1828 — Opens a general store, known as the Yellow Store, in Bethel.

1831 — Founds the *Herald of Freedom* newspaper and soon lands in trouble for criticizing important local people in its pages.

1835 — Purchases a slave, Joice Heth, and exhibits her as the 161-year-old former nurse of George Washington.

1841 — Buys Scudder's American Museum, at the corner of Broadway and Ann Street in New York City, and reopens it as Barnum's American Museum.

1842 — Charles Stratton, also known as General Tom Thumb, first appears on the Lecture Hall stage of the American Museum.

1844 — Barnum and Tom Thumb appear before Queen Victoria at Buckingham Palace in London.

1848 — Barnum begins construction of Iranistan, a mansion near Bridgeport, Connecticut.

1850 — Under contract to P. T. Barnum, the Swedish singer Jenny Lind tours the United States to packed concert halls.

1856 — Barnum is forced into bankruptcy after agreeing to a partnership with the owner of the Jerome Clock Company of New Haven, Connecticut.

1865 — The American Museum burns to the ground. In the same year, Barnum is elected as a representative in the General Assembly, of the Connecticut state legislature.

1867 — Barnum loses in his run for the U.S. Congress.

1871 — Barnum goes into partnership with William C. Coup and Dan Castello to establish P. T. Barnum's Grand Traveling Museum, Menagerie, and Circus.

1880 — Barnum forms a partnership with James Bailey and James Hutchinson, to establish the Barnum and London Circus, which begins touring in 1881.

1885 — Bailey quits his partnership with Barnum, selling his share to W. W. Cole and James E. Cooper.

1888 — James Bailey buys the shares of Cole, Cooper, and James Hutchinson, and with Barnum founds the Barnum & Bailey Circus.

1891 — P. T. Barnum dies in Bridgeport on April 7 at the age of 80.

1907 — The Ringling brothers buy the Barnum & Bailey Circus. They operate the shows separately until 1919, when they combine them into the Ringling Brothers and Barnum & Bailey Circus.

CHAPTER NOTES

CHAPTER 1
A Hoax

1. P. T. Barnum, *Barnum's Own Story: The Autobiography of P. T. Barnum* (Gloucester, Mass.: Peter Smith, 1972), p. 3.

CHAPTER 2
The Barnums of Bethel

1. A. H. Saxon, *P. T. Barnum: The Legend and the Man* (New York: Columbia University Press, 1989), p. 27.
2. Philip B. Kunhardt, Jr., Philip B. Kunhardt III, and Peter Kunhardt, *P. T. Barnum: America's Greatest Showman* (New York: Alfred A. Knopf, 1995), p. 12.
3. P. T. Barnum, *Barnum's Own Story: The Autobiography of P. T. Barnum* (Gloucester, Mass.: Peter Smith, 1972), pp. 12–13.
4. Morris Robert Werner, *Barnum* (New York: Harcourt, Brace and Company, 1923), p. 17.
5. Kunhardt, Kunhardt, and Kunhardt, p. 15.
6. Barnum, p. 38.
7. Saxon, p. 42.
8. Harvey W. Root, *The Unknown Barnum* (New York: Harper & Brothers, 1927), p. 45.
9. Saxon, p. 43.
10. Barnum, p. 42.

CHAPTER 3
George Washington's Nurse?

1. P. T. Barnum, *Barnum's Own Story: The Autobiography of P. T. Barnum* (Gloucester, Mass.: Peter Smith, 1972), p. 36.
2. A. H. Saxon, *P. T. Barnum: The Legend and the Man* (New York: Columbia University Press, 1989), p. 41.
3. Barnum, p. 84.
4. Philip B. Kunhardt, Jr., Philip B. Kunhardt III, and Peter Kunhardt, *P. T. Barnum: America's Greatest Showman* (New York: Alfred A. Knopf, 1995), p. 19; Barnum, p. 45.
5. Morris Robert Werner, *Barnum* (New York: Harcourt, Brace and Company, 1923), pp. 29–30.
6. Kunhardt, Kunhardt, and Kunhardt, p. 21.
7. Ibid., p. 20.
8. James W. Cook, ed., *The Colossal P. T. Barnum Reader: Nothing Else Like It in the Universe* (Chicago: University of Illinois Press, 2005), pp. 48–49.
9. P. T. Barnum, *Humbugs of the World* (New York: Carleton, 1866), pp. 12–13.
10. Barnum, *Barnum's Own Story*, p. 59.

CHAPTER 4
The American Museum

1. Morris Robert Werner, *Barnum* (New York: Harcourt, Brace and Company, 1923), p. 46; Harvey W. Root, *The Unknown Barnum* (New York: Harper & Brothers, 1927), p. 81.
2. A. H. Saxon, *P. T. Barnum: The Legend and the Man* (New York: Columbia University Press, 1989), p. 89.
3. Werner, p. 47.
4. Root, p. 85.

5. P. T. Barnum, *Barnum's Own Story: The Autobiography of P. T. Barnum* (Gloucester, Mass.: Peter Smith, 1972), p. 99.
6. LeRoy Ashby, *With Amusement for All* (Lexington: University Press of Kentucky, 2006), p. 38.
7. Barnum, p. 106.
8. Saxon, p. 102.
9. Barnum, pp. 124–125.
10. Bluford Adams, *E Pluribus Barnum: The Great Showman and the Making of U.S. Popular Culture* (Minneapolis: University of Minnesota Press, 1997), p. 100.
11. Werner, p. 56.
12. Barnum, p. 113.
13. Philip B. Kunhardt, Jr., Philip B. Kunhardt, III, and Peter Kunhardt, *P. T. Barnum: America's Greatest Showman* (New York: Alfred A. Knopf, 1995), p. 43.

CHAPTER 5
General Tom Thumb

1. Harvey W. Root, *The Unknown Barnum* (New York: Harper & Brothers, 1927), p. 97.
2. Morris Robert Werner, *Barnum* (New York: Harcourt, Brace and Company, 1923), p. 77.
3. A. H. Saxon, *P. T. Barnum: The Legend and the Man* (New York: Columbia University Press, 1989), p. 132.
4. A. H. Saxon, ed., *Selected Letters of P. T. Barnum* (New York: Columbia University Press, 1983), p. 32.
5. Philip B. Kunhardt, Jr., Philip B. Kunhardt, III, and Peter Kunhardt, *P. T. Barnum: America's Greatest Showman* (New York: Alfred A. Knopf, 1995), p. 62.
6. Ibid., p. 84.
7. Ibid., p. 82.
8. Ibid., pp. 82–83.

9. Bluford Adams, *E Pluribus Barnum: The Great Showman and the Making of U.S. Popular Culture* (Minneapolis: University of Minnesota Press, 1997), p. 42; Werner, pp. 118–119.
10. Kunhardt, Kunhardt, and Kunhardt, p. 94.
11. Neil Harris, *Humbug: The Art of P. T. Barnum* (Chicago: The University of Chicago Press, 1973), p. 119.
12. Adams, p. 59.
13. Harris, p. 145.

CHAPTER 6
Money Trouble

1. A. H. Saxon, *P. T. Barnum: The Legend and the Man* (New York: Columbia University Press, 1989), p. 192.
2. Ibid.
3. Philip B. Kunhardt, Jr., Philip B. Kunhardt, III, and Peter Kunhardt, *P. T. Barnum: America's Greatest Showman* (New York: Alfred A. Knopf, 1995), p. 122.
4. Saxon, p. 199.
5. P. T. Barnum, *Barnum's Own Story: The Autobiography of P. T. Barnum* (Gloucester, Mass.: Peter Smith, 1972), p. 270.
6. Saxon, p. 204.
7. Ibid., p. 207.
8. Ibid., p. 209.
9. Ibid., p. 210.
10. Ibid., p. 221.

CHAPTER 7
The Greatest Show on Earth

1. P. T. Barnum, *Barnum's Own Story: The Autobiography of P. T. Barnum* (Gloucester, Mass.: Peter Smith, 1972), pp. 401–402.

2. Philip B. Kunhardt, Jr., Philip B. Kunhardt, III, and Peter Kunhardt, *P. T. Barnum: America's Greatest Showman* (New York: Alfred A. Knopf, 1995), p. 239.

3. P. T. Barnum, *Struggles and Triumphs: or Forty Years' Recollections of P. T. Barnum* (Hartford, Conn.: J. B. Burr, 1869), p. 162.

4. Kunhardt, Kunhardt, and Kunhardt, p. 243.

5. Neil Harris, *Humbug: The Art of P. T. Barnum* (Chicago: The University of Chicago Press, 1973), pp. 249–250.

6. A. H. Saxon, *P. T. Barnum: The Legend and the Man* (New York: Columbia University Press, 1989), p. 282.

7. Harris, p. 257.

8. Barnum, *Barnum's Own Story*, p. 430.

9. Ibid., p. 443.

10. Saxon, p. 298

CHAPTER 8
The End of the Show?

1. Philip B. Kunhardt, Jr., Philip B. Kunhardt III, and Peter Kunhardt, *P. T. Barnum: America's Greatest Showman* (New York: Alfred A. Knopf, 1995), p. 296.

2. Ibid., p. 344.

GLOSSARY

Barnum & Bailey Circus—A show founded in 1887 with a partnership between James Bailey and P. T. Barnum. James Bailey became the sole owner of the show after the death of P. T. Barnum in 1891. The show was sold to the Ringling Brothers in 1907, becoming the Ringling Brothers and Barnum & Bailey Circus.

Cooper and Bailey Circus—A traveling show owned by James Bailey and James Cooper that competed with P. T. Barnum's traveling exhibitions during the late 1870s.

Herald of Freedom—A newspaper founded and edited by P. T. Barnum and published in Bethel, Connecticut, in the 1830s.

hippodrome track—An oval track placed outside the rings in a circus, and used for parades, races, and various spectacles.

humbug—A fraud or fake, exhibited or advertised to take advantage of the public.

Iranistan—Barnum's elaborate mansion near the town of Bridgeport, Connecticut, built in 1848 and destroyed by fire in 1857.

P. T. Barnum's Asiatic Caravan—A traveling exhibition, in which P. T. Barnum was a partner that toured from 1851 to 1854.

P. T. Barnum's and Great London Combined—A show that was created in 1880 with the new partnership of P. T. Barnum, James Bailey, and James L. Hutchinson.

P. T. Barnum's Grand Traveling Museum, Menagerie, and Circus—Also known as the Barnum Show, a circus established in 1870 by the partners P. T. Barnum, William C. Coup, and Dan Castello.

ring—A circular performance space, usually 42 feet in diameter (the dimension of a standard horse training track), used in circuses.

royalties—A payment to an author or artists of a percentage of sales of his or her work.

taxidermist—A person skilled in the preparation and mounting of dead animals for exhibition.

ventriloquist—A person able to speak without giving the appearance of talking.

FURTHER READING

Books

Apps, Jerry. *Tents, Tigers and the Ringling Brothers.* Madison, Wis.: Wisconsin Historical Society Press, 2007.

Farquhar, Michael. *A Treasury of Deception: Liars, Misleaders, Hoodwinkers, and the Extraordinary True Stories of History's Greatest Hoaxes, Fakes, and Frauds.* New York: Penguin, 2005.

Mierau, Christina. *Accept No Substitutes!: The History of American Advertising.* Minneapolis: Lerner, 2000.

Pascoe, Elaine. *Fooled You!: Fakes and Hoaxes through the Years.* New York: Henry Holt, 2005.

Standiford, Natalie. *The Stone Giant: A Hoax that Fooled America.* New York: Golden Books, 2001.

Warrick, Karen Clemens. *P. T. Barnum: Genius of the Three-Ring Circus.* Berkeley Heights, N.J.: Enslow Publishers, Inc., 2001.

Worth, Bonnie. *Jumbo: The Most Famous Elephant in the World!.* New York: Random House, 2001.

Internet Addresses

The Barnum Museum
    <http://www.barnum-museum.org/>

Circus Historical Society
    <http://www.circushistory.org/>

P. T. Barnum
    <http://www.ptbarnum.org/>

INDEX